PASS
Cambridge
BEC Higher

Ian Wood, Louse Pile *with* Sarah Curtis

MULTILINGUAL
WORD LISTS
ONLINE

NATIONAL
GEOGRAPHIC
LEARNING

CENGAGE
Learning·

Australia • Brazil • Japan • Korea • Mexico • Singapore • Spain • United Kingdom • United States

**Pass Cambridge BEC Higher Student's Book
Second Edition**
Ian Wood and Louise Pile *with* Sarah Curtis

Publisher: Jason Mann

Senior Commissioning Editor: John Waterman

Editorial Project Manager: Karen White

Development Editor: Sarah Curtis

Content Project Editor: Denise Power

Production Controller: Tom Relf

Marketing and Communications Manager:
  Michelle Cresswell

Head of Production and Manufacturing:
  Alissa McWhinnie

Compositor: MPS Limited, a Macmillan Company

Text Design: InPraxis

Cover Design: Maria Papageorgiou

ISBN: 978-1-133-31322-9

National Geographic Learning
Cheriton House, North Way, Andover, Hampshire, SP10 5BE
United Kingdom

Cengage Learning is a leading provider of customized learning solutions with office locations around the globe, including Singapore, the United Kingdom, Australia, Mexico, Brazil and Japan. Locate your local office at: **international.cengage.com/region**

Cengage Learning products are represented in Canada by Nelson Education, Ltd.

Visit National Geographic Learning online at **ngl.cengage.com**
Visit our corporate website at **www.cengage.com**

Acknowledgements

We are grateful to the following for permission to reproduce copyright material:

Belbin for the company logo and details on pages 13–14 by Barry Watson 2000. Reproduced with permission from Belbin, 2011; Professor Lynda Applegate for an extract on page 17 from "Time for the big small company" by Lynda Applegate, published in *The Financial Times*, 1 March 1999, copyright © Lynda Applegate. Reproduced with kind permission; The Financial Times for 'FT500 stock market listings' image on page 24, published in *The Financial Times*, 24 October 1999, copyright © The Financial Times Limited 2011. All rights reserved; Graphs on pages 26, 27 and 130 showing details from Tesco, Jan-April 2011; Marks and Spencer, November 2010–April 2011, Carphone Warehouse, November 2010–April 2011; Serabi, Feb 2011–May 2011; and Shanta Gold, February 2011–May 2011, www.lse.co.uk/, copyright © London South East; The Independent for an extract on page 29 from 'Danger in mergers. Just ask Lloyds TSB' by Jeremy Warner, 7 March 2009, copyright © The Independent, 2009; BP for their company logo on page 30. Reproduced with permission; RBS for the Natwest company logo on page 30. Reproduced with permission; GlaxoSmithKline for their company logo on page 30. Reproduced with permission; The National B2B Centre for the National B2B Centre logo and an extract on pages 54–55 adapted from 'What is e-business' The National B2B Centre website. www.nb2b.co.uk. Reproduced with permission; Forrester Research, Inc. for the graph on page 57 from 'US Online Retail Forecast, 2009 To 2014", Forrester Research Inc., March 5, 2010, copyright © Forrester Research, Inc.; The Telegraph for an extract on page 85 from 'Meeting the company's motivational challenge' by Adrian Furnham, *The Sunday Telegraph*, 25 October 1998, copyright © Telegraph Media Group Ltd, 1998; IKEA for their company logo, information and audio interview about IKEA on page 97. Reproduced with permission; Michael Segalla for an extract on page 101 adapted from 'National cultures, international business' by Michael Segalla, *The Financial Times*, 7 March 1998, copyright © Michael Segalla; Interbrand for the table on page 122 'World's top 10 brands by value, 2010', copyright © Interbrand; Professor JN Kapferer for an extract on page 123 adapted from 'Making brands work around the world' by Jean-Noël Kapferer, *The Financial Times*, 30 January 1998, copyright © JN Kapferer, Professor at HEC Paris. Author of "The new strategic brand management" (Kogan Page); adidas Group for their company logo on page 125. "adidas" and the "3-Bars logo" are registered trade marks of the adidas Group, used with permission; Research In Motion UK Limited for the Blackberry® logo on page 125. Reproduced with permission; Ford for their company logo on page 125. Reproduced with permission; Procter & Gamble for the Olay logo on page 125. Reproduced with permission; McDonalds Corporation for their company logo on page 125. Used with permission from McDonald's Corporation; and Nestlé® for their company logo on page 125. Nestlé and the "birds' nest" device are registered trademarks of Société des Produits Nestlé S.A., Vevey, Switzerland. Reproduced with permission.

In some instances we have been unable to trace the owners of copyright material and we would appreciate any information that would enable us to do so.

Photo Credits

Bernhard Classen/Alamy p16(b), Caro/Alamy p25, Fancy/Alamy p27, Paul Vidler/Alamy p38(t), Steve Nichols/Alamy p41, Iain Masterton/Alamy p38(b), David Gee 4/Alamy p39(t), EIGHTFISH/Alamy p42(tr), Ben Ashmole/Alamy p45(r), CCPhotography/Alamy p52(m), Nicholas Burningham/Alamy p53(bl), radharcimages.com/Alamy p53(br), Eric Carr/Alamy p53(bml), Jim Cartwright/Alamy p53(bmr), Michael Philip/Alamy p54(r), B.O'Kane/Alamy p56(t), NetPhotos/Alamy p56(br and bl), Goddard Automotive/Alamy p84, Steve Cukrov/Alamy p86, Zoonar GmbH/Alamy, Blend Images/Alamy p96, Alex Segre/Alamy p97(b and tm), Stuart Forster/Alamy p98(l), Greg Balfour Evans/Alamy p99(b) ; **Patti McConville/Getty** p12, Comstock/Getty p15, Andreas Kindler/Getty p18(tl), Digital Vision./Getty p18(tr), Paper Boat Creative/Getty p18(b), Comstock/Getty p26, Elliot Elliot/Getty p27, Reggie Casagrande/Getty p43(b), Michele Falzone/Getty p44(r), Yuji Kotani/Getty p44(l), Hisham Ibrahim/Getty p50, Stephen Marks/Getty p51(tl), Comstock Images/Getty p51(ml), Zero Creatives/Getty p51(r), Jack Hollingsworth/Getty p51(bl), Pando Hal/Getty p51, Dougal Waters/Getty p52(l), Getty Images p52(r), Roy Hsu/Getty p53(tl), Chabruken/Getty p53(tm), Daniel Allan/Getty p53, Pando Hal/Getty p53(tr), Rayman/Getty p54(b), Jetta Productions/Getty p57(l), Comstock/Getty p84(ml), Lin Yangchen/Getty p84, Stockbyte/Getty p84(mr), Colin Gray/Getty p84(b), Chase Jarvis/Getty p84(t), Dave & Les Jacobs/Getty p86, Jose Luis Pelaez Inc/Getty p86, Caroline von Tuempling/Getty p91(tl), Fisher/Thatcher/Getty p91(tr), Bloomberg/Getty pp97(t) and 99(tl), Digital Vision./Getty p100(l), Pankaj & Insy Shah/Getty p100(r), Ellinor Hall/Getty p112(b), Ellinor Hall/Getty p113(t), PhotoAlto/Eric Audras/Getty p116, Hans Neleman/Getty p117, Chicasso/Getty p124, Ray Kachatorian/Getty p127; Winhorse/Istockphoto p42(b), **Winhorse/Istockphoto** p42(tl), Troels Graugaard/Istockphoto p84, Kamo/Istockphoto p84, Tim Abramowitz/Istockphoto p84, kristian sekulic/Istockphoto p84,Joas Kotzsch/Istockphoto p110(t), Neil Kendall/Istockphoto p110(b), александр Стулов/Istockphoto p112(t), Doug Berry/Istockphoto p129; **Peter MacKinven/View Pictures/Rex Features** p98(r), SINOPIX/Rex Features pp97(bm) and 99(tr); **Cherniga Maksym/Shutterstock** pp38(ml) and 39, slavchovr/Shutterstock p38(m), Eky Studio/Shutterstock p38(mr), Ssguy/Shutterstock p42(m), Hfng/Shutterstock p44(m), Jan Kowalski/Shutterstock p45(l), Elena Elesseeva/Shutterstock p57(r), Kentoh/Shutterstock p114, Junker/Shutterstock p126.

Printed in Singapore by Seng Lee Press
Print Number: 04   Print Year: 2015

Introduction

The Cambridge BEC examination

The **Cambridge Business English Certificate (BEC)** is an international business English examination which offers a language qualification for learners who use, or will need to use, English for their work. It is available at three levels:

Cambridge BEC Higher
Cambridge BEC Vantage
Cambridge BEC Preliminary

Cambridge BEC Higher is a practical examination that focuses on English in business-related situations. The major emphasis is on the development of language skills for work: reading, writing, listening and speaking.

Pass Cambridge BEC Higher

The book contains:

- **Introduction**   An introductory unit which gives you information about the examination and this preparation course.

- **Core units**   Eight double units which cover a wide range of business-related topics. Many of the exercise types correspond to those in the examination.

- **Self-study**   A section following every double unit to provide consolidation of the language of the units and some examination-related tasks. It also contains a focus on a particular grammatical area to enable you to review your grammar systematically.

- **Exam practice**   Examination-style exercises following every double unit to provide further practice in the examination skills you will need.

- **Exam focus**   A section in the centre of the book to prepare you directly for the examination.

- **Audioscripts**   The content of the audio CDs.

- **Answer key**   Answers to Self-study and Exam practice.

Multilingual key vocabulary lists are available on our website at www.summertown.co.uk.

Language development in *Pass Cambridge BEC Higher*

- **Reading**

  Reading is the most tested skill in the examination. The book therefore contains a great deal of reading practice, using authentic, semi-authentic and examination-style texts. Do not panic if you do not understand every word of a text; sometimes you only need to understand the general idea or one particular part. However, you need to read very carefully when answering examination questions; sometimes the most obvious answer on the first reading is not correct and you will change your mind if you re-read the text.

- **Writing**

  In the examination you have to write letters and reports and also describe trends. You need to ensure that you fulfil the task while observing the word limit. If you have good spoken English, it does not necessarily mean that you can write well; to be successful, you need training and practice.

- **Listening**

  Listening is also a very important skill for the examination and most units contain listening activities. You can find the **Audioscripts** to the audio CDs at the back of the book.

- **Speaking**

  You can find help on how to prepare for the Speaking Test in the **Exam focus** section. In addition, there are speaking activities in every unit.

- **Vocabulary**

  Although vocabulary is tested explicitly only in Reading Test Part Four, it is very important throughout the examination. Many exercises in the **Self-study** sections recycle vocabulary from the units.

- **Grammar**

  A grammatical point is covered in most units. Moreover, grammar is systematically reviewed in the **Self-study** sections of the book. However, the review is brief and you may need to supplement the material.

- **Optional tasks**

  At the end of most units there is an optional task for you to do between lessons, the aim of which is to integrate your studies with real-world activities. For example, you may be asked to visit a company's website and write a report on your findings.

Examination preparation in *Pass Cambridge BEC Higher*

- **Introduction**

    The **Introduction** presents the content of the examination and important examination dates.

- **Core units and Self-study**

    All units contain at least one examination-style exercise and there are also some examination-related tasks in the **Self-study** sections.

- **Exam practice**

    Each double unit is followed by at least two pages of **Exam practice**, which supplement the examination practice in the core units and **Self-study**. Complete Listening Tests follow Units 4 and 8. By the end of the book, you will have practised every part of the examination several times.

- **Exam focus**

    The **Exam focus** section in the centre of the book gives you information about how to succeed in each part of the examination. The Writing and Speaking Test Assessment Sheets provide a framework for you to evaluate your own writing and speaking skills.

Contents   Language   Exam Skills

	Language	**Exam Skills**

Introduction

Cambridge Business English Certificate Higher

All Cambridge BEC Higher candidates receive a statement of results showing their overall grade (Pass grades A, B, C or Fail grades D, E) and their performance in each of the four papers. Look at the following extract from a sample statement.

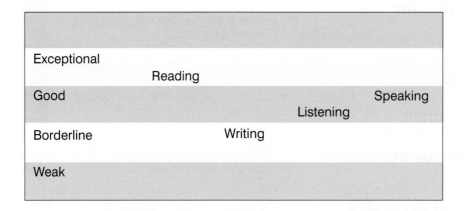

Exceptional	
	Reading
Good	Speaking
	Listening
Borderline	Writing
Weak	

Successful candidates receive a certificate showing a single grade. Each paper represents 25% of the total mark.

An overview

The following table gives an overview of the different parts of the examination, how long they take and what they involve.

	Test	Length	Contents
1	Reading	60 minutes	Six parts
2	Writing	70 minutes	Two parts (short description of a graph, formal letter, short report or proposal)
3	Listening	40 minutes	Three parts Approx. 15 minutes of listening material played twice plus time to transfer answers
4	Speaking	16 minutes	Three parts (personal information, short talk and collaborative task) Two examiners and two or three candidates

Important Cambridge BEC Higher dates

Your teacher will give you some important dates at the start of your course. Write these dates in the boxes below.

Cambridge BEC Higher examination

Your teacher will give you the dates of the written papers but can only give you the date of the Speaking Test after your entry has been confirmed by Cambridge.

- PAPER 1 Reading & Writing Test

- PAPER 2 Listening Test

- Speaking Test (to be confirmed)   Between   and

Entry date

This is the date by which the examination centre must receive your examination entry.

- Entries must be confirmed by

Grades and certificates

Cambridge sends out results approximately seven weeks after the examination. Successful candidates receive their certificates about four weeks after that.

- Results should be available by

Preparing for Cambridge BEC Higher

1 Look at the following activities which you are going to do on your BEC Higher course. Which two are you most confident about? Which two are you least confident about? Why?

- answer questions on business-related texts
- focus on the structure and organisation of texts
- proof-read short texts

- describe graphs
- write formal letters
- write short reports

- complete notes from presentations
- identify the main ideas from short extracts
- answer questions based on interviews

- talk about yourself and your job
- discuss problems and reach agreement
- give short talks

- review grammar structures
- expand general business vocabulary
- learn useful phrases for writing and speaking

2 Which of these are useful for your current job or may be useful in the future?

Quiz: Pass Cambridge BEC Higher

1 Where would you find the following in this book? Write the unit or page numbers.

1 Information from a famous furniture retailer

2 A list of the top ten global brands

3 An exercise on articles

4 An audioscript of a presentation by a headhunter

5 Advice on writing reports

6 An exercise about linking words and phrases

7 A questionnaire about your job

8 Advice on the language of agreeing and disagreeing

9 Helpful tips for each of the Cambridge BEC Higher papers

10 A card exercise focusing on the language of trends

11 A **Self-study** vocabulary exercise on mergers

12 A checklist to help you evaluate your writing

Helping yourself succeed

1 Look at the areas below. Add further ideas for using your time outside lessons to help you improve your English skills. How could each activity help you in the exam?

Reading

Reading English language newspapers

Writing

Listening

Speaking

Speaking to my foreign colleagues in English

Language

Work roles

Describing work roles

Speaking

1 Work in pairs. Find out the following information about your partner.

- position
- responsibilities
- duties

Reading 1

2 Read the brochure extract on the opposite page from the management consultancy Belbin Associates. How does the WorkSet system use colour to clarify work roles?

3 Look at the following pie charts and the WorkSet extract. How does the manager's brief compare with what the employee actually does?

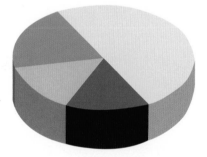

Manager's brief to the employee

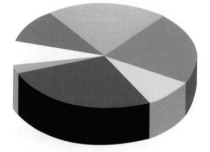

Employee's feedback on the job

4 A manager assigns the following tasks to different workers. Match each verb with one of the four core WorkSet colours.

| schedule | support | operate | design | co-operate |
| assist | participate | comply | decide | follow |

Think of another verb for each core colour.

What is WorkSet?

WorkSet is an advanced means of setting up jobs and developing employees in response to the changing nature of work. By adopting the use of colours, companies can specify the exact level of responsibility to be allocated to the key tasks that form an employee's job description. WorkSet replaces the often static job description with a more dynamic short-term job brief.

The employee interprets the manager's brief and uses it as a framework for approaching the tasks that make up the job. A feedback and review process then enables the manager to keep abreast of what the employee actually does and provides an opportunity to jointly assess performance, re-align the job and decide on the development needs of the employee.

Core colours

BLUE WORK refers to tasks an employee has to carry out in a prescribed way to an approved standard. Example: machining an engineering component to a specification.

YELLOW WORK involves personal responsibility for meeting an objective. Exactly how the work is done does not matter too much as long as the goal is achieved. Example: initiating procedures to reduce costs by 15%.

GREEN WORK refers to tasks that vary according to the reactions and needs of others. Example: helping the hotel service manager at times of peak occupancy.

ORANGE WORK involves shared rather than individual responsibility for achieving an objective. Example: contributing to a management team.

Employee feedback colours

GREY WORK refers to work which is incidental to the job and involves responding to situational needs. Example: being asked to entertain a visitor.

WHITE WORK refers to any new or creative undertakings outside the employee's formal duties which may lead to improvements. Example: revising standard customer service letters.

PINK WORK demands the presence of the employee but serves no useful purpose. Example: attending meetings where nothing new is learnt and no contribution to decision-making is encouraged.

Listening 🔘 1.01–1.05

5 **Five people talk about their jobs. Listen and decide which improvement each speaker would most like to see.**

1 .....
2 .....
3 .....
4 .....
5 .....

A more responsibility

B more teamwork

C fewer routine tasks

D more flexible hours

E fewer interruptions

F clearer objectives

G more creative work

H more managerial support

Language

6 Look at the present simple and present continuous forms in the following sentences. Find further examples of these forms in the audioscript and discuss how they are used.

*I **work** for the UK subsidiary of a Japanese company.*
*I**'m working** for a small leisure group on a one-year contract.*

Speaking

7 Work in pairs. Use WorkSet to produce a pie chart describing your partner's job.

Report writing

Reading 2

1 Barrie Watson of Belbin Associates has just led a Team Leadership Workshop at Ekstrom Engineering. Read his report on the workshop. How did he use WorkSet?

Report on Effective Team Leadership Workshop

The aim of this report is to summarise issues arising from the recent Team Leadership Workshop at Ekstrom and recommend appropriate action.

Findings
The workshop began with an assessment of how the Ekstrom team leaders understood their roles. Perceptions ranged from assigning and checking other people's work to motivating others to do the work. This disparity clearly showed that the team leaders had different understandings of their roles and that Ekstrom therefore needed to communicate its expectations more explicitly.

In order to do this, Ekstrom identified key tasks and used WorkSet colours to illustrate the precise level of responsibility which could be allocated to each. A task such as communicating with the team, for example, might be approached in a variety of ways:

- I give my staff instructions every morning. (Blue work)
- I let my staff decide on the best approach for themselves. (Yellow work)
- My team and I discuss how to do each job. (Orange work)

Having identified the different possible approaches to each key task, the company was able to select which was most appropriate and communicate its expectations in terms of the skills and behaviour required.

Conclusions
It is clear that Ekstrom needs to ensure that its team leaders are capable of performing key tasks in a manner compatible with company expectations. However, whilst the appropriate skills can be developed through in-company training, changing behavioural attributes is much more difficult.

Recommendations
We strongly recommend, therefore, that Ekstrom sets up assessment centres where existing team leaders and new applicants can be screened to ensure that they have the appropriate attributes for effective team leadership.

Barrie Watson
Belbin Associates

3-4 Bennell Court, Comberton, Cambridge CB3 7DS,
Telephone: 01223 264975, Facsimile: 01223 264976, email: belbin@belbin.com

2 **Read the report again and answer the following questions.**

    1 What were the team leaders asked to do first?

    2 What did this show?

    3 What did the use of WorkSet colours then allow the company to do?

    4 Why does Barrie Watson distinguish between skills and attributes?

    5 How can Ekstrom ensure its team leaders have the right attributes?

3 **Complete the following information with phrases from the report.**

Don't forget

Report writing

The following phrases are useful when writing reports.

- **Introduction**
  This report aims/sets out to ...
  _____

- **Findings**
  It was found that ...
  _____

- **Conclusions**
  It was decided/agreed/felt that ...
  _____

- **Recommendations**
  It is suggested that ...
  _____

Writing

4 **Use WorkSet colours to compare your job brief with how you actually spend your time at work. Write a 200–250 word report describing your findings and recommending any necessary changes. Consider the following.**

- the title of the report
- the heading and content of each paragraph
- useful phrases for each paragraph

Company structure

Types of company structure

Speaking

1 Look at the following diagrams. What kind of company structure do you think each one represents?

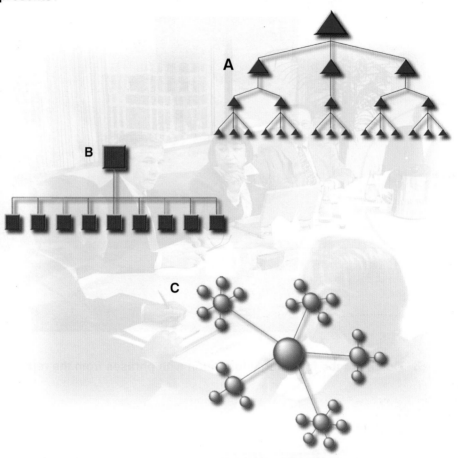

Reading

2 Read the article on the opposite page. What are the advantages and disadvantages of each company structure?

3 Read the article again and answer the following questions.

1 What is the difference between operating and management processes?

2 How do hierarchical companies ensure control of operating systems?

3 How can entrepreneurial companies be responsive and retain control?

4 Why does information alone not guarantee effective management?

Time for the big small company

With speed increasingly seen as the key to competitive advantage, the dream is to marry the control of an established company with the responsiveness of a start-up. As Lynda Applegate reports, advances in IT now mean that the 'big small' company is finally feasible.

In the hierarchical companies of the 1960s and 1970s, information moved slowly and channels of communication were limited. Over the past few years, however, large companies have come
5 under ever-increasing pressure to collect, process and distribute information more quickly in order to compete with smaller, more nimble rivals. The key challenge facing any sizeable organisation today is how to achieve responsiveness without losing the control inherent in a
10 hierarchical structure.

All types of organisation are controlled through two sets of processes. Operating processes define how a company produces, sells, distributes and supports its products and services. Management processes define
15 how a company directs, coordinates and controls these operations. Typical management processes include planning, budgeting and human resource management.

Traditional hierarchical organisations control operating processes through standardisation of jobs.
20 These jobs are separated into sequential steps and carried out under direct supervision. However, the line workers lack both the authority and motivation to improve these routine tasks and are limited by their local view of the business. Management processes in such companies
25 are also hampered by the time it takes to recognise that change is needed. Thus, hierarchical control is only truly effective in relatively stable business environments where change happens slowly.

Entrepreneurial organisations, on the other hand, allow
30 fast response without any loss of control. Daily personal interaction between the owner and employees ensures flexibility and responsiveness, while instant feedback ensures effective control. However, as the company becomes larger and more complex, this control breaks
35 down and more structured operating and management processes are required.

Information age organisations can manage the complexity of the large hierarchical structure without losing the speed of the entrepreneurial start-up. IT plays a critical role. It co-ordinates complex fast-cycle operating 40 processes and, more importantly, gives decision-makers quick access to detailed, real-time information about operations and market performance. Once all this information is flowing, employees can quickly evaluate their decisions and continually refine both strategy 45 and operations. Organisational control then becomes a dynamic, information-enabled learning process rather than a static monitoring system.

However, although IT makes the 'big small' company possible, it cannot motivate people to use information in 50 order to act on behalf of the organisation. The challenge for organisations is therefore to ensure that managers and employees share the same perspective on the business and are motivated to accomplish the same goals.

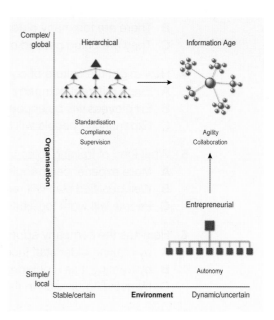

Adapted from the *Financial Times*

Speaking   4 Which of the structures is most like the organisation you work for?

Flexible working

1 Don McNally, from Brennar Manufacturing, an engineering company based in the north of England, talks about how changes to retirement age will affect his company. Listen and say whether he is looking forward to the changes and why.

2 Listen again and choose one letter for the correct answer.

Don McNally
Brennar Manufacturing

1 What is the main effect these changes will have on businesses?
 A that the age of retirement will change
 B in the administration of people's retirement
 C in the number of people not wanting to retire

2 How many people will need to be re-assigned?
 A almost everyone over the age of 65
 B precisely 81% of cases
 C fewer than 20% of those reaching retirement age

3 How does this affect younger employees?
 A They are not getting the experience they need.
 B There are too many older people at work.
 C They are being passed over for promotion.

4 How might the culture of companies change?
 A Every different company will find a different solution.
 B Employees will be encouraged to share experience.
 C Experienced people will be redeployed into training roles.

5 What kind of training roles are likely to be applied?
 A More experienced people will mentor younger colleagues.
 B Well-qualified staff will receive more formal training.
 C People will work together in specific roles.

6 How has the company approached implementing change?
 A by making older staff face up to it
 B by treating it as a personal problem
 C by avoiding division in the workforce

7 What has been the effect of people working in these teams?
 A They have learned to respect each other more.
 B People have begun to share their skills and practices.
 C Managers are able to resolve conflict better.

8 What does Don see happening in the future?
 A The principle of team working will be applied to other areas.
 B The workforce will become increasingly flexible.
 C Team working will increase productivity.

Language

3 Look at the tenses in the following sentences. Find further examples of these forms in the audioscript and discuss how they are used.

*Several years ago we **changed** our company policy so that ...*
*The young **have been acquiring** the working habits of their older colleagues.*
*There **has been** some reluctance on the part of individuals.*

Speaking

4 Work in pairs. Use the Brennar questionnaire to assess the suitability of your partner for redeployment into a training or mentoring role. What other factors would be important?

Redeployment Questionnaire

BRENNAR ENGINEERING

Please complete the questionnaire and use it in discussion with your line manager.

Q1 How many years experience do you have in your job?

5–10 years	10–15 years	15–20 years	20+ years	at Brennar	elsewhere

Q2 How do you assess your ability in the following?

	Poor	Average	Good	Excellent
Communicating with colleagues				
Dealing with problems				
Discussing work with managers				
Planning work				
Delegating tasks				

Q3 How often in a week do you tell or show colleagues how to do something?

daily	2–3 times	once	less than once

Q4 What do you feel that your experience can offer less experienced colleagues?

_____

_____

_____

Writing

5 Write a 200–250 word report assessing the suitability of yourself or your partner for redeployment in a training or mentoring role. Separate the report into logical paragraphs with appropriate headings.

Optional task

6 Visit www.asda.jobs, the recruitment website of a large retail chain in the UK. What do they value about their employees, and how do they aim to build a team spirit in their workforce?

1 Choose the correct word to fill each gap.

Research has shown that in today's dynamic working environment the traditional job description is no longer doing its job. Today's jobs are not (1) _____ – they are constantly changing. This leads to (2) _____ , with employees uncertain of their precise work roles. This can be illustrated by the following quotation from a job description: 'Meet or exceed customer (3) _____ .' The initial reaction may be that this (4) _____ is perfectly clear but on closer examination it poses a number of questions. For example, is it (5) _____ employees to do whatever they feel is necessary to (6) _____ this end without restrictions? Or is it saying (7) _____ our procedures and this will be the outcome? Who knows? Perhaps the manager, but the description certainly does not (8) _____ things sufficiently from the employee's point of view.

1	A static	B routine	C standard
2	A disparity	B initiative	C ambiguity
3	A undertakings	B objectives	C expectations
4	A schedule	B feedback	C statement
5	A authorising	B allocating	C prescribing
6	A support	B achieve	C carry out
7	A follow	B comply	C serve
8	A highlight	B identify	C clarify

2 Use the words to write sentences with *job*.

He re-aligned certain aspects of the job.

carry out

aspects   brief

highlight

communicate   responsibilities

description   (**job**)   classify

feedback   monitor

re-align

set up   enjoy

duties

3 Use the prompts to write sentences to be included in a formal report.

1 'There's a lack of communication in Sales.'
(*it/feel*) _It was felt that there was a lack of communication in sales._

2 'Let's organise some training for our team leaders.'
(*it/suggest*) _____

_____

3 'We're going to bring in a consultant.'
(*it/decide*) _____

_____

4 'It seems team leaders' roles aren't clear enough.'
(*it/find*) _____

_____

5 'OK, we'll start implementing WorkSet next month.'
(*it/agree*) _____

_____

6 'Ekstrom needs to set up new assessment centres.'
(*we/recommend*) _____

_____

Present simple and continuous

4 Complete the email. Put each verb in brackets into the correct form of the present simple or continuous.

Sally

Colin (**1** *want*) _wants_ a meeting on Friday morning at 10.30 to discuss ways of improving team leadership within the company. I know we usually (**2** *hold*) _____ our weekly sales briefings then but Colin (**3** *say*) _____ this is more important. He's worried that our team leaders (**4** *not/delegate*) _____ anywhere near enough responsibility and that could be the reason why the atmosphere (**5** *not/seem/get*) _____ any better around here. Colin must be pretty worried because he (**6** *even/bring*) _____ in a consultant. Remember the guy we had in the summer? Well, I (**7** *think*) _____ it's the same one again, so he should be good. Some of the things he showed us last time about time management were really useful. As a result, I (**8** *definitely/get*) _____ a lot better at prioritising my work nowadays. Anyway, I'd better go.

See you on Friday.

Bob

Self-study 1b

1 Match the words as they appear in the unit.

1	support	intranet
2	virtual	services
3	corporate	manager
4	line	organisation
5	business	support
6	hierarchical	environment
7	online	costs
8	operating	team

2 Complete the table.

Verb	Noun	Adjective
standardise	_____	_____
_____	diversity	_____
_____	_____	responsive
_____	operation	_____
_____	_____	suitable
_____	supervision	_____
_____	_____	varied

3 Which word in each group is the odd one out?

1	collaborative	remote	team-based	co-operative
2	stable	static	sequential	routine
3	responsive	dynamic	flexible	virtual
4	separate	divide	specify	break down
5	back up	resist	hamper	prevent
6	evaluation	feedback	interaction	assessment
7	accomplish	challenge	manage	achieve
8	strategy	concept	impact	plan
9	paperwork	hard copy	email	stationery
10	motivation	authority	control	supervision

4 Complete each sentence with a suitable preposition.

1 The company is separated _____ several different business units.

2 People come together _____ a specific purpose and then go on to join new teams.

3 Some managers worry that staff can only work if they're _____ direct supervision.

4 I spend most of my day working _____ the company network.

5 Some people find it hard to cope _____ working from home.

6 Management should encourage staff to use information _____ behalf of the organisation.

5 Some of the following lines contain an unnecessary word. Underline any extra words in lines 1–13.

1 Many firms now offer home-based working opportunities
2 to their staff as those demands for more flexible
3 arrangements grow. Companies such like the BBC, for
4 example, are running schemes where managers,
5 journalists, producers and accountants all have work from
6 home. The manager of one project said, 'It is popular with
7 all staff. They are lot happier, use their time more
8 productively and are less stressed. They are saving money
9 by not commuting and can spend themselves more time
10 with their families.' He also mentioned the need for
11 home-based staff and to be able to cope with technology.
12 'Good information technology support is the absolutely
13 crucial to the success of any home-working scheme.'

Past simple and present perfect

6 Complete the conversation. Put each verb in brackets into the correct form of the past simple, present perfect simple or present perfect continuous.

● Linda, (1 you/hear) *have you heard* the news?

▼ What news?

● They (2 just/promote) _____ Sue to Head of European Sales.

▼ Sue? You must be joking! She (3 not/even/work) _____ for the company all that long. When (4 she/join) _____ , about last May? Anyway, who (5 tell) _____ you about it?

● Maurice. I (6 see) _____ him yesterday at the International Sales Conference. Yes, apparently Sue (7 break) _____ all kinds of records since she (8 look) _____ after the Central European Region.

▼ But I always (9 think) _____ Francesco (10 be) _____ in line for that position.

● Well, it seems Sue (11 make) _____ a huge impression on the board and they're worried they might lose her. Maurice says that headhunters (12 already/call) _____ on a pretty regular basis so ...

▼ And what about poor Francesco? How (13 he/take) _____ the news?

● I don't really know. Maurice (14 not/mention) _____ Francesco at all. But I guess he'll be pretty disappointed. He's certainly made no secret of the fact that he wanted the job.

Reading Test Part One

- Look at the sentences below and the profiles of five international executives.
- Who does each sentence refer to?
- For each sentence **1–8**, mark **one** letter **A, B, C, D or E.**
- You will need to use some of the letters more than once.

Example

0 He was once involved in national politics.

---

1 He has cut operating costs by reducing the number of senior staff.
2 He does not enjoy making presentations and speeches.
3 He started his career working for a television station.
4 He improved the company's financial position by selling off assets.
5 He is expanding the company with a series of takeovers.
6 He is famous for his imagination and tough business strategies.
7 He has been with the same employer all his working life.
8 He has worked in a variety of different industries.

A

Michael Martins, *Chairman, Ecofoodsmart*

Michael Martins has recently returned to Ecofoodsmart, the large retail food chain, after a 20-year absence. Whilst away, he held a variety of posts in local government including that of mayor for six years, where his skills as an effective public speaker won him great respect. He then returned to the industry as one of the two architects behind the dramatic revival of the Remco supermarket chain. His comprehensive and varied experience of the retail food sector will make a huge impact on Ecofoodsmart and he has already embarked on an ambitious policy of major acquisitions.

B

Steven Waugh, *Chief Executive Officer, DigiCom*

Steven Waugh, the driving force behind DigiCom for over 25 years, retires this year. Known for his quick decision-making, he is seen as one of the most outspoken and ruthless operators in the world of business. These qualities have often made life difficult for DigiCom competitors, who have regularly been faced with bitter price wars and innovative promotional campaigns, often masterminded by the CEO himself. Born in Queensland, Waugh first cut his teeth on Australia's Channel 9 before entering broadcasting in Britain. Never a great believer in political correctness, he is famous for spending his time aboard his luxury cruiser indulging in gourmet food and champagne.

C

Mark Boucher, *Chairman, Gladstone*

Mark Boucher, 53, chairs Gladstone, the base-metals group recently demerged from Corgen of South Africa and floated in Amsterdam. Since the breakaway, Gladstone's operating profit has grown to $92m, even though experts have described the company as overstaffed and inefficient. Boucher is a reserved man who is reluctant to address large meetings but reveals, when pressed, a dry sense of humour. He has had an unusual career path, including a spell working for the North American Space Agency, followed by a stint running a satellite TV station.

D

> **Erik Johanssen,** *Chief Executive, MorgenReynolds*
> MorgenReynolds' CEO Erik Johanssen admits to crying occasionally and says he is not the tough hard-nosed businessman that people expect when they meet him. He is, however, universally regarded as a shrewd politician within the industry. A self-styled company man, the chain smoking 55 year-old Johanssen has been with Morgen for over 20 years. Since Morgen took over the innovative but under-performing Reynolds, Johanssen has streamlined the business radically, axing half of Reynolds' top managers. Johanssen lives modestly in Stockholm and travels to work by underground.

E

> **Joe Anderson,** *Chief Executive, Dayton International Hotels*
> Joe Anderson joined the imaginative Seattle-based Foyles restaurant chain after graduating in 1973. He worked his way up through the ranks, performing a variety of different roles, eventually becoming the Managing Director in 1986 and joining the parent company's executive board in 1990. In 2004 he became CEO and President of the group's Dayton International Hotels division. Anderson has focused on Dayton's core restaurant and hotel activities and reduced the group's debts by disposing of several properties and a chain of beauty salons. His next project is likely to be the search for strategic alliances with major European hotel chains.

Reading Test Part Five

- Read the article below about an ageing workforce.
- For each question **1–10**, write **one** word.

Example

0 | W | E | L | L | | | | |

Working beyond retirement

An increasing number of people are choosing to work beyond the traditional retirement age of 65. There are a variety of reasons for this. For many it is a financial necessity, but for others the workplace offers social contact with like-minded people as (**0**) ..... as the chance to keep mentally active.

A recent survey shows that the number of people expecting to work beyond (**1**) ..... planned retirement age has increased (**2**) ..... 57% in 2010 to 62% in 2011 and the aim of the report is to show (**3**) ..... this will impact (**4**) ..... society. With the abolition of the state retirement age, many people in the UK will continue to work for longer, with more than half saying they would consider staying in employment, either full or part-time in return for (**5**) ..... higher retirement income.

Over the past ten years the number of people working beyond state pension age has risen by 30% and according to official figures women are (**6**) ..... most likely to be found working beyond the state retirement age, due to their generally lower earnings.

A similar picture (**7**) ..... emerging in the US with (**8**) ..... than 25% of the population working beyond the age of 65 and (**9**) ..... to 14% still working past 70. Many more want to work, but face age discrimination. Yet these 'greying' workers want to learn new skills (**10**) ..... as teaching or even truck driving to keep active in their communities and remain mentally alert.

Stocks and shares

Share prices

Speaking **1** Where can you find out about a company's share price?

Reading **2** Look at the following extract from the FT500 stock market listings. Match the letters a–f with the explanations below.

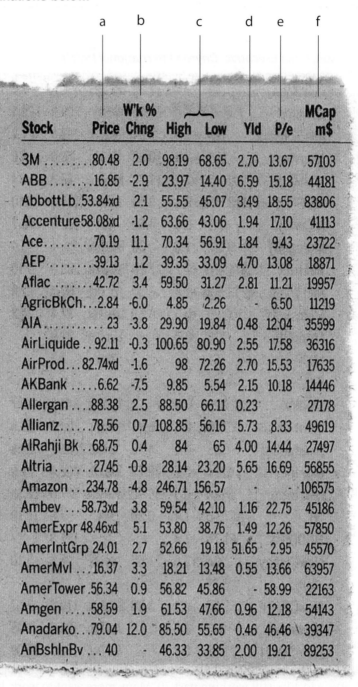

Stock	Price	a W'k % Chng	b High	Low	c Yld	d P/e	e MCap m$ f
3M	80.48	2.0	98.19	68.65	2.70	13.67	57103
ABB	16.85	-2.9	23.97	14.40	6.59	15.18	44181
AbbottLb	53.84xd	2.1	55.55	45.07	3.49	18.55	83806
Accenture	58.08xd	-1.2	63.66	43.06	1.94	17.10	41113
Ace	70.19	11.1	70.34	56.91	1.84	9.43	23722
AEP	39.13	1.2	39.35	33.09	4.70	13.08	18871
Aflac	42.72	3.4	59.50	31.27	2.81	11.21	19957
AgricBkCh	2.84	-6.0	4.85	2.26	-	6.50	11219
AIA	23	-3.8	29.90	19.84	0.48	12.04	35599
AirLiquide	92.11	-0.3	100.65	80.90	2.55	17.58	36316
AirProd	82.74xd	-1.6	98	72.26	2.70	15.53	17635
AKBank	6.62	-7.5	9.85	5.54	2.15	10.18	14446
Allergan	88.38	2.5	88.50	66.11	0.23	-	27178
Allianz	78.56	0.7	108.85	56.16	5.73	8.33	49619
AlRahji Bk	68.75	0.4	84	65	4.00	14.44	27497
Altria	27.45	-0.8	28.14	23.20	5.65	16.69	56855
Amazon	234.78	-4.8	246.71	156.57	-	-	106575
Ambev	58.73xd	3.8	59.54	42.10	1.16	22.75	45186
AmerExpr	48.46xd	5.1	53.80	38.76	1.49	12.26	57850
AmerIntGrp	24.01	2.7	52.66	19.18	51.65	2.95	45570
AmerMvl	16.37	3.3	18.21	13.48	0.55	13.66	63957
AmerTower	56.34	0.9	56.82	45.86	-	58.99	22163
Amgen	58.59	1.9	61.53	47.66	0.96	12.18	54143
Anadarko	79.04	12.0	85.50	55.65	0.46	46.46	39347
AnBshInBv	40	-	46.33	33.85	2.00	19.21	89253

1 change in share price compared with previous week

2 amount paid out to shareholders for each dollar invested

3 total market value of all of a company's shares

4 price of shares at close of previous day's business

5 highest and lowest prices during previous day

6 price/earnings ratio (current share price divided by earnings per share)

Speaking

3 **How common is investing in shares in your country?**

Market trends

Listening 1 **1** **Listen to a television report about share prices of retail companies. How have they performed over the last three months?**

7 pista   (1.07)

2 **Listen again and choose one letter for the correct answer.**

1 What drove up the price of retail shares?
   A Increased growth in market share.
   B The profitability of the businesses.
   C The fact that demand for shares has exceeded supply.

2 How profitable are retail businesses?
   A They are generally very profitable.
   B It depends on market share.
   C It depends on the price of shares.

3 Investors are attracted to retail companies because
   A the market is expanding.
   B they are businesses they know.
   C the businesses have been around for a long time.

4 Which companies have remained successful?
   A the discount end of the market
   B the newer companies
   C the larger companies

5 What was the immediate effect of the financial crisis?
   A There was a loss of confidence.
   B The banks closed down.
   C There was a sell-off in shares.

6 Why did share prices fall?
   A Retailers diversified too much.
   B There was a fall in confidence and spending.
   C Confidence fell.

7 Katie thinks that share prices will
   A rise and fall a little.
   B lead to profits.
   C remain stable.

8 There is the possibility of
   A discount sellers repositioning themselves.
   B share prices falling for ever.
   C long term profits for investors.

3 **Would you be prepared to invest in retail shares? Why/Why not?**

Describing graphs

Speaking

1 **The graph shows the price for Tesco shares over a three-month period. Your teacher will give you some cards. Describe the graph using all the words on the cards.**

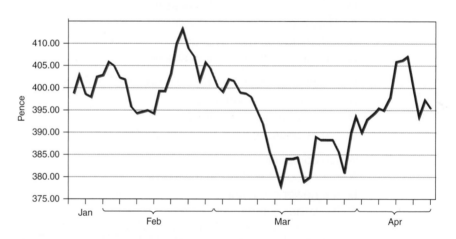

Listening 2 **2** **Now listen to a description of the graph. In what order are the cards used?**

1.08

Language **3** **Look at the audioscript and find examples of the following.**

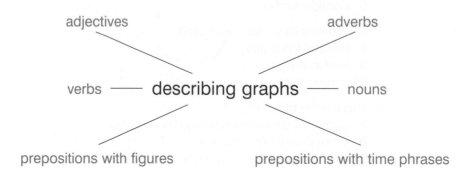

Don't forget

Writing

4 Look at the share prices of Marks and Spencer and The Carphone Warehouse over a six-month period. Write a 120–140 word report comparing the performance of the two shares.

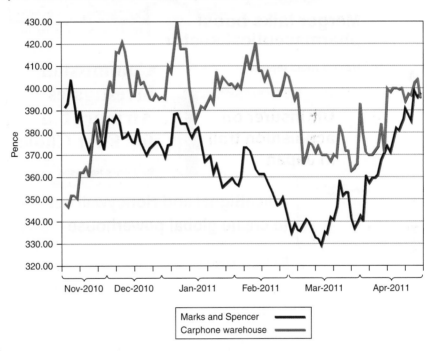

Optional task

5 You have $10,000 to invest in shares. Use the listings in the financial press or on the internet to buy and sell shares. Check the progress of your investments during your course. Can you make more profit than the interest on a standard savings account?

Mergers and acquisitions

Understanding mergers

Speaking

1 Why do companies merge with or acquire other companies? What problems can arise?

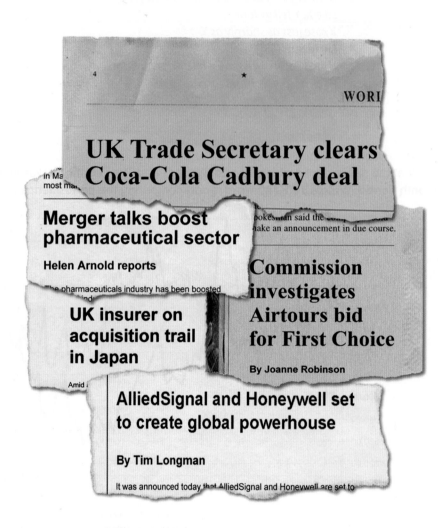

Reading

2 Read the article on the opposite page about mergers and acquisitions. What successes and problems are mentioned?

Successes	Problems

Danger in mergers. Just ask Lloyds TSB

Outlook: Has any takeover or merger ever produced long-term value for investors and other stakeholders?

There must be cases of it, though it is hard to think of them, and many recent examples seem only to have succeeded in wiping out the bidding company almost entirely. Lloyds TSB's disastrous acquisition of HBOS is another case in point.

Even the chief executive, Eric Daniels, now admits he probably could have avoided taking any Government money but for the HBOS takeover. Most of the rubbish he's now being forced to put into the Government's asset protection scheme comes from HBOS.

The upshot is that the Treasury ends up with a 75 per cent economic interest in the combined entity, diluting original Lloyds TSB shareholders down to a tiny fraction of their original interest. In hindsight, this is almost as bad a deal as Sir Fred Goodwin's acquisition of the 'toxic' bits of ABN Amro, which similarly holed Royal Bank of Scotland below the waterline, forcing it to fall back on the tender mercies of the politicians.

Just to complete the hat-trick, HSBC finally got round to admitting this week what everyone else has known since the start – that the acquisition back in 2002 of the US sub-prime lender Household International was a mistake. HSBC is so big it still seems unlikely Household will end up destroying the mother ship, but it's already done untold damage and there is undoubtedly more to come.

Ironically, one of Sir Fred's former acquisitions, that of National Westminster Bank in 2000, is generally regarded as a model takeover which did succeed in creating lots of value. Yet the point is that NatWest didn't have to be taken over by a tiny little Scottish upstart to succeed: it only needed to be managed a bit more effectively. What's more, the success Sir Fred achieved with NatWest plainly went to his head and greatly contributed to the hubris which eventually did for RBS.

That's one of the other problems with takeovers. If by any chance they do succeed, the emperor who created the resulting behemoth nearly always ends up overstaying his welcome, with the result that eventually the rot sets in and mistakes are made. Lord Browne, who was formerly chief executive of BP, was a classic example of it.

A series of mega-mergers succeeded in re-establishing BP's footprint as one of the world's leading oil majors, yet standards of safety and operational efficiency were allowed seriously to slip. Lord Browne was eventually forced out by personal scandal, but the ship was listing badly by the time he left. His successor found much of the necessary integration had yet to be done.

Both Vodafone's takeover of Mannesmann at the turn of the century and Glaxo Wellcome's merger with SmithKline Beecham around the same time succeeded in creating a couple of very big companies, but even now, all these years later, they have failed to add a penny to shareholder value. To the contrary, it can reasonably be argued that they destroyed it.

All academic research shows most takeovers don't work, in the sense that they fail to create any value for the bidding company. In many cases, the resulting clash of corporate cultures can kill the organisation stone dead. So why do companies keep doing them?

Pursuit of monopoly is one reason, and provides the best rationale for the Lloyds takeover of HBOS. But it nearly always turns out to be illusory, and monopolists never succeed in keeping an acquired dominant market position. The most charitable explanation is that M&A is another form of industrial restructuring which allows the corporate landscape to evolve and change. Mergers may not create value, but it is certainly possible that many of these companies would be in even worse shape on their own. Yet it's debatable. Takeovers are what companies do when they mature, or when managements have run out of ideas for creating new growth opportunities. They are more the result of executive boredom than imaginative thinking.

Financial engineering, or asset stripping, is another major motivation, particularly among the takeover kings of private equity. This purpose too has turned to dust in the downturn of the past couple of years. It only works when there are plentiful quantities of credit around to produce the leverage, and, in any case, its consequences for investment and jobs are frequently far from benign.

But the main explanation is our old friends the investment bankers, who seem to be the root of all ills these days. They provide both the wherewithal to make takeovers happen and the almost invariably flawed logic behind them. Managements are made to feel inadequate unless they are also fee-paying deal-makers.

The only consistently successful deal-makers in my experience are individuals acting in their own self-interest and therefore able to look beyond the siren calls of the investment bankers. Empire-building bosses of public companies do not on the whole make good takeover kings. Few takeovers work out as they are supposed to, and not infrequently they end up destroying the whole company.

3 **Read the article again and choose one letter for the correct answer.**

1 Lloyds' merger with HBOS was a mistake because
   A the government had to intervene.
   B HBOS has a large number of bad debts.
   C Lloyds paid too much into the merger.
   D shareholders' interests were diluted.

2 HSBC's acquisition of Household International
   A gave them a position in the US market.
   B was the third merger of its kind.
   C has damaged the business.
   D was only recently announced.

3 NatWest needed
   A to be taken over to succeed.
   B to be downsized to succeed.
   C to create more value to succeed.
   D to have better management to succeed.

4 How are mergers said to be bad for companies?
   A The companies clash in their operations.
   B They rarely create any additional value.
   C Corporate culture may damage the business.
   D They kill organisational efficiency.

5 What is the most likely reason for mergers and acquisitions?
   A To provide the illusion of monopoly.
   B To find new opportunities for growth.
   C To dominate the market.
   D To enable a company to mature.

6 The most successful deal-makers
   A work in partnership with investment banks.
   B are trying to build business empires.
   C need banks to provide the wherewithal to make things happen.
   D are investors acting for themselves.

Language

4 **Look at the article again and find examples of the following.**

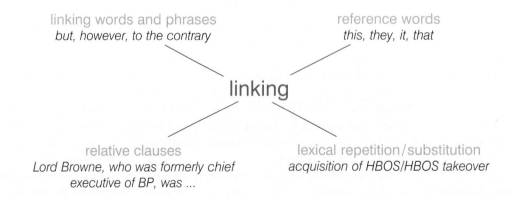

linking words and phrases
but, however, to the contrary

reference words
this, they, it, that

linking

relative clauses
Lord Browne, who was formerly chief executive of BP, was ...

lexical repetition/substitution
acquisition of HBOS/HBOS takeover

Speaking

5 **Think of a recent merger or acquisition. What were the reasons behind it?**

Why merge?

1 Jason Labone from Hinton and Bailey, an economic research consultancy, is speaking at a conference called to discuss current economic trends. He has prepared a handout summarising his talk for his audience. Listen and complete the notes with up to three words.

Hinton & Bailey

Introduction

1 These observations have been made during the course of my work providing _____ data for businesses in the UK.

2 The talk will discuss the reasons for the recent _____ of mergers and acquisitions and look at how they differ from those which took place before the financial crisis of 2008.

Reasons for increase in M and A

3 There has been a noticeable _____ in the majority of industries since the onset of recession.

4 With markets in a downturn, it has become more difficult for businesses to find opportunities for _____ .

5 In the financial sector, larger businesses have become _____ , while smaller players have struggled with increased costs.

6 Smaller financial institutions have found it necessary to merge as the industry goes through a _____ .

Changes in M and A since 2008

7 Since 2008, banks are feeling pressure to move the economy out of recession, now that they have been _____ by government.

8 Now more cautious with risk, banks are only making finance available where mergers are seen to make _____ for the industry.

9 Those interested in the takeover of Cadbury were _____ , rather than private equity firms.

10 Deals like this one are seen as _____ with a greater likelihood of growth in the long term.

Prospects for the future

11 Banks and other financial institutions are likely to lend _____ , in areas where risk can be managed more easily.

12 Mergers and acquisitions are likely to be funded by private _____ to a greater extent than they were before 2008.

Speaking

2 Your company wants to merge with or acquire another company. Discuss the following.

- which company to merge with or acquire
- the benefits that would result

Optional task

3 Write a brief profile of a recent merger. Include information about its size, products and markets.

1 Match the following words with the diagrams.

recover	general upward trend	peak
fluctuate	level off	bottom out

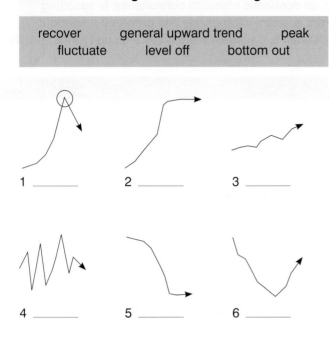

1 _____   2 _____   3 _____

4 _____   5 _____   6 _____

2 Complete the text with the following words.

broker	merger	commission	dividends
listings	flotation	investment	shares

The first time I ever bought (**1**) _____ was in 1988. It was during the (**2**) _____ of British Telecom. I didn't really know anything about the stock market but a friend of mine is a (**3**) _____ and he told me BT would be a safe (**4**) _____ . Since then, he's also taught me all about how to read the (**5**) _____ in the financial press. Of course, I pay him some (**6**) _____ but I think he gives me a lot more help than he would a normal client. He'll phone me, for example, if he hears a rumour about a (**7**) _____ or a takeover. He also gives me good information about companies, such as who pays their shareholders the biggest (**8**) _____ and things like that. His advice doesn't guarantee success, of course, but it's certainly a great help.

3 Do the following statements refer to positive (↑), negative (↓) or neutral (→) trends?

1 We operated at break-even point for most of 2009.

2 Prices really began to take off early this year.

3 The over-supply of shares depressed the markets.

4 Performance of the shares exceeded all expectations.

5 The markets showed investors' lack of confidence.

6 None of the analysts predicted the collapse.

7 Merger rumours caused share prices to shoot up.

8 Prices fluctuated but remained fairly steady overall.

4 Write a 120–140 word report comparing the monthly sales of *Fresh 'n' Cool* with those of the previous year.

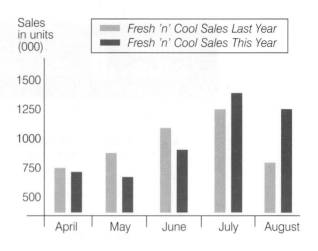

Describing trends

5 The graph shows the share price of two companies from 2006 to 2010. Find and correct any mistakes in the text.

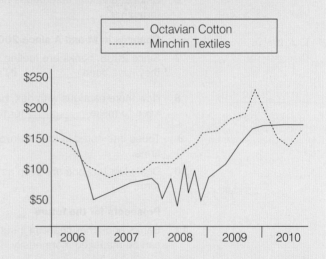

In the start of 2006, shares in Octavian Cotton stood at $160. However, by the end of the year they have collapsed to just $50. They recovered steady over the next twelve months but have fluctuated sharply all through 2008. In 2009 they continued their recover, climb to $160 per share, where they remained throughout 2010.

Shares in Minchin Textiles starting trading at $150. Like Octavian, Minchin saw it's shares fall during 2006 and then picked up the following year. This recovery then turns into a general upward trend, what continued until late 2009, when shares peaked at $220. They then collapsed before rise briefly to just over $150 at the end of 2010.

1 Read the article on page 29 again and put the following companies into the correct groups.

> ABN Amro   BP   GlaxoWellcome
> HBOS   Household International   HSBC
> Lloyds TSB   Mannesmann
> National Westminster Bank
> SmithKline Beecham
> Royal Bank of Scotland   Vodafone

Acquired another company	Merged with another company	Was acquired by another company
		HBOS

Find examples of words that are joined with a hyphen. Put them into two groups. How are the words in one group different from the other?

2 Complete the sentences with the correct form of the following words.

> grow   restructure   merge   takeover
> benefit   compete   streamline   acquire

1 The telecoms sector was rocked when Vodafone launched a hostile _____ bid for Mannesmann.

2 After _____ with an Italian company, we had to re-assess our language training needs.

3 The chairman told shareholders that accepting the offer would lead to long-term _____ in sales.

4 The merger will help us to secure a _____ advantage over our biggest rivals.

5 There is no doubt that the merger will deliver substantial cost _____ .

6 To fight a hostile bid, the company announced plans to _____ the workforce by cutting 2000 jobs.

7 The move led to a major _____ programme, especially in duplicated areas such as administration.

8 After a period of major expansion through _____ , we began to lose focus of our core activities.

3 Match the words as they appear in the unit.

1	achieve	operating	of scale
2	integrate	economies	value
3	add	different	prices
4	undercut	cost	improvements
5	reduce	long-term	cultures
6	generate	competitors'	costs

4 Fill each gap with a suitable word.

Advanced Technologies plc, the automobile components manufacturer, yesterday agreed (**1**) _____ consider an offer from the French-based Avignon Group of 108p a share. This latest bid, which (**2**) _____ an increase of 13p on their original offer, beats (**3**) _____ of German rival Hellman AG, who last week offered 101p a share. The bid values Advanced at £28m, almost twice (**4**) _____ market capitalisation when it was floated in 2007. It is not yet clear (**5**) _____ Hellman will return with a counterbid. Advanced Chairman Tom McGillis said the company would (**6**) _____ contact any other parties for two weeks (**7**) _____ it considered Avignon's newest offer. An Avignon spokesman said that the merger would deliver immediate benefits to the company (**8**) _____ as cost savings and long-term sustainable shareholder value.

Relative pronouns

5 Complete the text by filling each gap with a suitable relative pronoun. Add any necessary commas.

The merger raises a number of HR issues (**1**) _which/that_ will need to be addressed as a matter of urgency and in a manner (**2**) _____ is seen to be fair to the employees of both companies. Firstly the pay structures of the two companies (**3**) _____ show marked differences will need to be reviewed and harmonised. Furthermore redundancy terms will have to be agreed and offered to employees (**4**) _____ lose their jobs as a result of the merger. This is particularly important with regard to senior managers (**5**) _____ contracts contain severance clauses (**6**) _____ guarantee them generous terms. Our approach to these job cuts (**7**) _____ were promised to shareholders as part of the terms of the merger will also have a major effect on staff morale within the newly-formed company. It is imperative that we avoid any deterioration of staff morale (**8**) _____ could have an adverse effect on company performance.

Reading Test Part Two

- Read the letter replying to an enquiry about conference facilities.
- Choose the best sentence from **A–H** to fill in each of the gaps.
- For each gap **1–6**, mark one letter **A–H**.
- Do not use any letter more than once.
- There is an example at the beginning (**0**).

Dear

I was delighted to meet you at the UK Conference Exhibition last week in Bath and I would like to take the opportunity to thank you for the interest you have shown in the wide range of conference centres we represent. **0** **H** Photographs of our superb centre can be viewed on our website at www.devonshiremanor. co.uk.

Devonshire Manor is set in 100 acres of private woodland and gardens approximately 10 miles south of Exeter city centre and just seven miles from the M5 motorway. **1** Despite the changes, Devonshire Manor has managed to retain the atmosphere of a traditional English country estate.

Devonshire Manor provides the ideal venue for both conferences and meetings of up to 40 delegates. **2** These gardens are an immensely popular setting for functions such as open-air press conferences and product launches. The meeting rooms themselves are completely self-contained, with full air-conditioning and sound-proofing. **3** Flip charts, whiteboards, TVs and high speed Internet are all included as standard. Photocopying facilities are also available at an extra cost.

Devonshire Manor has 20 en suite bedrooms, all of which are beautifully furnished and contain a writing desk, colour TV, free wireless connection telephone and minibar. We hope that delegates find time to enjoy the wealth of activities which both the Devonshire Manor estate and its surroundings have to offer. **4** After a hard day's work, such leisure facilities provide guests with the perfect opportunity to unwind.

Delegate rates start at £125 pp + VAT, based on 24-hour mid-week occupancy. **5** The price also includes parking and unlimited use of the leisure facilities during your stay at Devonshire Manor. **6** Alternatively, if you would like to discuss your particular requirements with us in more detail, we would be pleased to meet you. In the meantime, if you have any questions regarding the above information, please do not hesitate to contact me on (01392) 548697.

I look forward to hearing from you.

Yours sincerely

A For a quotation for your company's proposed conference, please complete the enclosed form.

B This is the reason why we give all delegates access to computer projector LCD and other visual aids.

C In addition to the house itself, there is also a beautiful terrace overlooking award-winning grounds.

D The large 17th century house has been tastefully renovated and refurbished to provide all the amenities of a modern conference centre.

E An extensive range of conference equipment is provided in each one.

F In addition to a nine-hole golf course, Devonshire Manor has four tennis courts, an outdoor heated swimming pool and a sauna.

G This covers the use of conference rooms and standard equipment as well as full-board accommodation.

H In response to your enquiry regarding Devonshire Manor, I enclose full details concerning the facility.

Reading Test Part Four

- Read the memo below about sales people's performance.
- Choose the best word to fill each gap.
- For each question **1–10**, mark one letter **A**, **B**, **C** or **D**.
- There is an example at the beginning (**0**).

Salesperson of the month

Our salesperson of the month is Kurt Steiner from Stuttgart, who wins four bottles of the finest champagne. Kurt achieved sales worth €150,000, which means that he (**0**) ..... his monthly target by over €40,000. Congratulations Kurt!

There was another excellent performance in Switzerland from Cécile Fourget, who almost won the prize on account of her (**1**) ..... high sales figures throughout June. Another Swiss salesperson with very good (**2**) ..... in June was Marie Dupont, with total sales of more than €130,000.

After a bad start to the month, sales in London (**3**) ..... swiftly, mainly due to the superb performance of Mike McGillis. Mike was successful in winning a major (**4**) ..... with LTV Production, which will be worth over €120,000 for the company.

In France, Claudette Le Blanc from Lyon sold €70,000 worth of business. This will obviously go a long (**5**) ..... towards increasing the turnover of one of our newest sites, which has been forced to (**6**) ..... at a loss for the last six months. Our Lisieux centre has also done well, with one of the newest (**7**) ..... of our French sales team, Jérome Zola, selling €50,000 worth of business.

As for Finland, our (**8**) ..... figures suggest that sales are well down compared to the same period last year. However, we expect that the situation will (**9**) ..... quickly once the recession is over.

Finally, just a reminder that our bonus scheme runs until the end of this week, so get your (**10**) ..... out to clients as quickly as possible. Who knows, you might be our next 'Salesperson of the month'!

Example

0   **A** exceeded   **B** excelled   **C** overtook   **D** overcame

A   B   C   D

■ □ □ □

1	**A** usually	**B** regularly	**C** consistently	**D** evenly
2	**A** levels	**B** results	**C** grades	**D** marks
3	**A** recovered	**B** regained	**C** restored	**D** repaired
4	**A** commission	**B** agreement	**C** contract	**D** arrangement
5	**A** route	**B** distance	**C** run	**D** way
6	**A** manage	**B** act	**C** operate	**D** work
7	**A** members	**B** delegates	**C** associates	**D** partners
8	**A** immediate	**B** actual	**C** instant	**D** current
9	**A** increase	**B** improve	**C** enlarge	**D** elevate
10	**A** statements	**B** invoices	**C** charges	**D** accounts

Reading Test Part Five

- Read the article below about industrial action at a bank.
- For each question **1–10**, write **one** word.

Example

0 | T | H | E | | | | | |

Bank says strike fails to make impact

Newham Bank and two major finance unions were fighting a war of words yesterday over the impact of a long-running pay dispute. A spokesman for the BBU, **(0)** ..... larger of the two unions, claimed that a second 24-hour strike **(1)** ..... had a serious impact on the bank's operations and that support for industrial action was growing. An estimated 28,000 staff walked out on Wednesday, causing **(2)** ..... the union called 'serious disruption'.

These claims, however, have been branded **(3)** ..... 'nonsense' by Newham. The bank said that fewer than 100 branches had closed **(4)** ..... of a total of over 1,500 and that the number of people taking part in the strike had been only about 4,000. The bank also denied claims by the unions that the action had put as **(5)** ..... as half its 2,000 cash machines out of service and caused delays to mortgage and loan authorisations.

'We're delighted at having had **(6)** ..... a great response from members,' said BBU official Amanda Conroy. 'There's absolutely **(7)** ..... doubt that this is having a very serious impact on Newham's operations.' The bank, on the other hand, said, 'The strike has had little or no impact on services in most areas of the country and almost **(8)** ..... our 56,000 staff are working as normal.'

The dispute began when the bank announced plans to implement a performance-based pay scheme, **(9)** ..... the unions maintain will lead to an effective pay freeze for 25,000 of **(10)** ..... members. However, the bank insists that the new scheme is a fairer way of rewarding hardworking employees.

Reading Test Part Six (A)

- In **most** lines of the following text, there is one unnecessary word. It is either grammatically incorrect or does not fit in with the sense of the text.
- For each numbered line **1–12**, find the unnecessary word. Some lines are correct. If a line is correct, write **CORRECT**.
- The exercise begins with two examples **(0)** and **(00)**.

Example

0 | C | O | R | R | E | C | T | | |

00 | T | H | I | S | | | | | |

Newsletter

0   Just one year after moving into the suburbs of Stockholm, our largest
00 Swedish branch this has outgrown its current premises. The centre will be
1   moving again in the next few weeks, this time order to purpose-built
2   offices in the city centre. Business has grown by more than a fifty per cent
3   during the past year. Moreover, the branch has recently been gained a
4   prestigious new contract with one of the city's major accountancy firms,
5   currently outsourcing its management training. The contract which will
6   initially be for a two-year period but we hope it will be extended. What
7   helped us win the contract was in the success of the training we have
8   been doing for similar companies in the recent years. Even though it is not
9   yet clear how big the contract will be, but it is expected to grow steadily
10 as more and more management training is gradually outsourced. We are
11 positive the excellent new location will be provide further boosts, both to
12 sales and morale. We would like to take this chance to thank you staff and
    management for their efforts over the last twelve months.

Reading Test Part Six (B)

- In **most** lines of the following text, there is **one** unnecessary word. It is either grammatically incorrect or does not fit in with the sense of the text.
- For each numbered line **1–12**, find the unnecessary word. Some lines are correct. If a line is correct, write **CORRECT**.
- The exercise begins with two examples (**0**) and (**00**).

Example

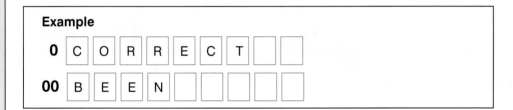

0 | C | O | R | R | E | C | T | | |

00 | B | E | E | N | | | | | |

0   One of the most effective ways to learn a language is to take a course in
00 the country where it is been spoken. That is why more and more
1   business and professional people they are attending language training
2   courses overseas rather than in their own country. Although such courses
3   may be expensive, participants have the opportunity to work on
4   developing their skills every minute of the day. In addition to have formal
5   lessons, participants have the opportunity to learn in social situations with
6   trainers and fellow students. Staying with a host family that gives
7   participants even more of exposure to the target language and helps them
8   make immediate use of the language they have learned. A course
9   overseas not only gives to participants the perfect way of experiencing the
10 cultural life of the country at a first hand. It also provides an opportunity for them
11 to make network with their counterparts and gain valuable insights which
12 will help them for operate more effectively in the global arena which is
    international business today.

Trade fairs

Exhibiting at a trade fair

Speaking

1 What are the benefits of trade fairs for exhibitors and visitors?

Reading 1

2 Read the advertisement. What details are given about the following?

| the exhibition | the exhibitors | the visitors |

28th–29th October 2011 • The NEC Birmingham
Friday & Saturday 09.30–17.30

Can you afford to miss this year's Festival of Ceramics?

The Festival of Ceramics is the leading ceramics event in Europe, with a growing following from Asia. Celebrating its twenty-third year, this is THE event for companies to showcase their creative designs to a worldwide audience of buyers.

This year over 400 companies will be in Birmingham to display their new products. For buyers this offers a unique opportunity to see the full range on offer in the ceramic community today and to meet the people responsible for providing the designs of the future.

Each company that attends the show has been selected to ensure that you, the buyer, will be able to see products which are both practical and inspirational. Whether you are interested in specialist,

highly individual ceramic pieces or more practical, mainstream products this is the show to keep you ahead of the competition.

The exhibition at the NEC attracts 30,000 UK and international quality buyers, suppliers and professionals from across the world who attend to see what new, interesting products are on offer and to network, develop and expand within the consistently growing creative ceramics industry.

More than fifty exhibitors will be attending The Festival of Ceramics for the first time this year, giving buyers a unique chance to meet the people who will be making tomorrow's headlines.

Show Features include:

• **FREE** Workshops featuring the latest products.
• **FREE** Business Seminars highlighting current topics.
• *Leading Pavilion* showcasing new designers.

3 **Your company wishes to exhibit at a trade fair. Discuss and decide the following.**

- your objectives for the trade fair
- where and when you should exhibit

Replying to an enquiry

1 **What information might trade fair organisers include in a standard letter of reply to enquiries about an exhibition?**

2 **Your teacher will give you the Festival of Ceramics' standard reply to enquiries. Put the sentences into the correct order. Then divide the letter into paragraphs.**

3 **Now read the Festival of Ceramics letter and compare your answer.**

28th–29th October 2011
The NEC Birmingham

Dear

Thank you for your interest in the 2011 Festival of Ceramics show. As requested, I enclose full details of this and future shows for you.

Held in Birmingham the Festival of Ceramics attracts buyers who understand the importance of good design and practical products. The Festival allows you to meet customers, old and new, face to face, in an atmosphere that allows you to show your products to their best advantage.

Now in its twenty-third year, the Festival of Ceramics remains the largest UK-based exhibition for ceramics. From the smallest egg cups to the largest pots for the garden, all can be found here at this exciting exhibition. So, whatever your ceramic products there will be a place for them. The exhibition has been attracting over 30,000 UK and overseas buyers since it moved to the NEC three years ago. Buyers who attend come from independent retailers, department stores, mail order houses and internet traders. If these are the people you need to meet, you will not be disappointed.

The key to the continuing popularity of the Festival of Ceramics is its selection of exhibitors, ensuring that buyers are seeing the very best in the industry. In addition to workshops, business seminars and shows, we give support to people in the industry, enabling them to make the right decisions .

Festival of Ceramics is always oversubscribed and by the time this letter reaches you, many of the available stands will already have been rebooked. Therefore, we recommend you reserve your stand as soon as possible and we guarantee all applications will be given our full attention the moment we receive them.

If you require any further information or advice, please do not hesitate to call Alex Whittle or myself on 0118 9784332 or email us on info@festivalofceramics.com

I look forward to hearing from you.

Best wishes

Liz Copping

Liz Copping
Sales Manager

4 **Look at the letter again and find examples of the following.**

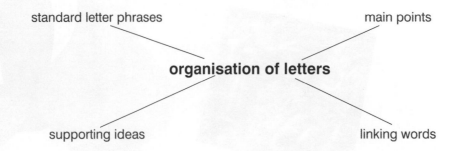

standard letter phrases   main points

organisation of letters

supporting ideas   linking words

Language

5 Look at the following sentence. Find further examples in the letter of the present simple referring to future time.

All applications will be given our full attention the moment we receive them.

6 Complete the following information with phrases from the Festival of Ceramics letter.

Don't forget

> **Standard letter phrases**
>
> The following phrases are useful when writing letters.
>
> ● **Referring to an earlier letter or conversation**
> *With reference to your letter dated ... in which ...*
> *Further to our conversation of ...*
> _____
>
> ● **Enclosing**
> *Please find enclosed ...*
> _____
>
> ● **Offering assistance**
> *Should you have any further questions,*
> *please contact me on ...*
> _____
>
> ● **Referring to future contact**
> *We look forward to meeting you on ...*
> _____

Writing

7 Write a 200–250 word letter of reply to an enquiry received by your company. Give details about the company's products/services and prices. Consider the following.

- who the reader is and what information is needed
- the purpose, order and content of paragraphs
- your main points and supporting ideas in each paragraph

Optional task

8 Research a trade fair of interest to your company. Write a 200–250 word report describing the event and recommending why your company should exhibit there.

Entering a market

Researching a market

Speaking

1 What research would a company do before entering a foreign market?

Reading

2 Read the text on the opposite page. Where might you find an article like this? Who is the text aimed at?

3 Read the text again and answer the following questions.

1 Why is the UK so important to China?
2 Which industries in China offer most potential for UK companies?
3 What can cause problems for companies attempting to do trade with China?
4 Which qualities are necessary for success in China?
5 Why is it advisable for exporters to visit China?

中英携手共创未来

Doing business in China

With one of the world's fastest rates of economic growth and a population of about 1.34 billion, China is an ideal market to do business with. UK exports to China hit a record high in September last year, reaching £743 million. Although imports from China in the same month reached £2.6 billion, the increase in exports came as good news to UK companies who had seen a reduction in their sales to the Asian giant in the preceding year. The Olympics in 2008 provided a valuable bridge between Beijing and London, with UK firms playing a key role in the design and engineering work on the Olympic stadia, as well as the new airport terminal. Now in 2011 the UK is continuing to encourage both export and import businesses with China.

The UK's strengths match China's needs, particularly in electrical and mechanical equipment, financial services, environmental and aviation technology and vehicles. Between July and September 2010 the overseas sales of trucks and aircraft parts pushed exports to China past the £2 billion mark for the first time ever. Opportunities exist for an ever increasing number of UK companies, yet many fail as they do not put sufficient time and effort into understanding some fundamental differences between the two cultures. Success in China is possible, but will require long-term commitment and the ability to research the market.

Thousands of British companies have achieved a great deal in China, initially in the south, but now throughout the country. However there are a number of strategies for working with the Chinese market and it is vital to recognise the importance of the differences between the Western and Eastern ways of doing business. Ignorance of these cultural differences underlies many misunderstandings arising from business negotiations. Building relationships with prospective business partners is vital for the most successful commercial transactions. Virtually all transactions in China result from the careful cultivation of the Chinese partner by the foreign one, until a relationship of trust evolves. Earning respect is essential and once a successful relationship has been established, commercial transactions will follow. Take time to get to know your prospective business partner, go to trade fairs, visit factories and find a reliable Chinese ally to work with you. An effective Chinese colleague will often be able to work out who in the other negotiating team holds real power, not always the boss, and help smooth out any possible problems. It will almost always be necessary to visit the market and the presence of a Westerner should also be exploited to the full. Chinese businessmen will often see a visit by a foreigner as an indication of sincerity and commitment by the Western company.

Language

4 Look at the articles (*a*, *an*, *the*) in the text. What main differences do you notice between the use of articles in English and your language?

Speaking

5 Choose one of the topics below and talk about it for one minute. Before you begin, think about the following.

- how to research a new export market
- the importance of good preparation for a business trip

| main points | supporting ideas | introduction | conclusion |

Business practices in China

1 Tanya Liddell, a successful exporter, addresses a local business association about doing business in China. Listen and complete the notes using up to three words or a number.

1	**On arrival in China**	There are few universally accepted business norms in China as _____ vary throughout the country.
2		It is essential to do thorough _____ before visiting China.
3		It is viewed as extremely rude if you are _____ in China.
4		When travelling from your hotel, always take into account the severe _____ _____ in Chinese cities.
5	**Meetings**	Upon arrival, you will normally be met by a _____ and fellow staff.
6		First of all, everyone exchanges _____ with one another.
7		The host will then formally open the meeting with a _____ to the company and its operations.
8		Visitors should notify their hosts in advance if they intend to use _____ _____ .
9	**Socialising**	Chinese hosts usually organise a _____ for foreign visitors.
10		A good topic of conversation is to enquire about your host's _____ _____ .
11		The Chinese feel an obligation to provide_____ at all times.
12		They will often arrange _____ for visitors.

2 What advice would you give Chinese people visiting your country on business?

Writing

3 You have received the following letter from a business acquaintance in China. Read the letter and write a 200–250 word reply.

ONCHINA
中国

21 June 2011

Floor 1A
Beijing Commercial Centre
9 Chang Road, Beijing
China

Dear

I do not know if you remember me but we met at the RC Mandarin Hotel in Shanghai last month. You gave me your business card and kindly offered to help me if I ever planned to visit your country.

I am pleased to say I will be attending a trade fair in your city next month. I am in the process of making my travel arrangements and, as it is my first trip to your country, I would appreciate it if you could give me some advice.

In particular, I would welcome your advice on accommodation and how to get around the city. Should I arrange car hire, for example? Also, as I will have my evenings free, could you recommend places to eat? I will have a free day for sightseeing as well. What would you suggest I do?

I hope we can meet during my visit. I would very much like to invite you for a meal one evening if it is convenient.

Thank you again for your help. I hope to hear from you soon.

Regards

Chen Zhang

Optional task **4** Look at a travel website. Choose a destination and prepare a brief presentation on where to stay, what to do and where to eat there.

1 Some of the following lines contain an unnecessary word. Underline any extra words in lines 1–14.

1 With a reference to your letter dated 13 November,

2 in which you requested information about our

3 forthcoming exhibition 'Management in Action',

4 please do find enclosed details about this and

5 future events in the region. 'Management in Action'

6 which is the showcase event for the region's major

7 business training organisations. This year's exhibition

8 it includes 30 free taster workshops, covering

9 these areas such as motivation, health and safety,

10 team-building, presentation skills and e-commerce.

11 If you require any further information, and please

12 do not hesitate to contact either myself or Elizabeth

13 Wellington on 01952 345642. We are look forward to

14 hearing from you in the near future.

2 Complete the puzzle. Which words run vertically through the answers?

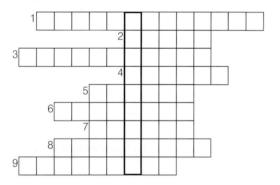

1 Organisers can promote an exhibition by placing an _____ in a newspaper or magazine.

2 Exhibition organisers often respond to enquiries with a standard letter of _____ .

3 Companies interested in exhibiting have to complete an _____ form and send samples.

4 The _____ of the stand and publicity material needs to fit in with our corporate image.

5 Earls Court hosts many top international _____ throughout the year.

6 One of the main _____ for exhibitors is the chance to meet customers face to face.

7 Exhibition organisers often reserve a number of _____ for first-time exhibitors.

8 Buyers come from independent _____ as well as large department stores.

9 At an exhibition, visitors can see the actual goods rather than just photos in _____ .

3 Re-arrange the words to make formal phrases from written correspondence.

1 enclosed / please / find
Please find enclosed

2 letter / of / to / reference / with / your
_____

3 look / meeting / we / forward / to / you
_____

4 to / our / conversation / further / of
_____

5 further / questions / should / have / you / any
_____

6 not / do / please / me / hesitate / contact / to
_____

Time clauses

5 Complete the conversation. Put each verb in brackets into the correct form.

● Hi Ross, it's Jan. I hear (**I** you/go) _you're going_ to the trade fair in Poznan next week.

▼ Yes. How about you?

● No, I'm not. But Monica's asked me to give you some details about travel arrangements and so on.

▼ Oh right, great.

● Do you have a pen ready?

▼ Sure, fire away.

● Right. Your plane (**2** land) _____ at Poznan at 10.20 on Thursday. It's flight BA442. When you (**3** get) _____ there, you'll be met at the airport by Sergiusz Jablonski.

▼ Will I be going into meetings as soon as I (**4** arrive) _____ or am I going to the hotel first?

● Sergiusz (**5** take) _____ you to your hotel. Once you (**6** check in) _____ , he'll take you to lunch with some of the managers.

▼ Ok. Is there anything planned for the evening?

● I'd imagine so, but they haven't sent us any details. I'm sure Sergiusz will let you know what's going on when you (**7** get) _____ there.

▼ OK. Let's see now. Is there anything else I need to know before I (**8** go) _____ ?

● I think that's about it. Your return flight's at 11.55 the next morning, so you'll have plenty of time to have a relaxed breakfast and make your way to the airport in good time.

1 Find words in the unit which go after business.

Business _partners_

_____

_____

_____

_____

_____

_____

_____

2 Complete the sentences with the following words.

amount to	respond to	enquire about
allow for	participate in	intend to
invest in		build on

1 Many UK financial service companies are particularly keen to _____ China.

2 Ensure that you warn your hosts in advance if you _____ use audio-visual equipment.

3 This year direct UK exports to China are estimated to _____ well over £1bn.

4 Having entered China, many UK companies are now looking to _____ their success.

5 When entering the Chinese market, a company has to _____ regional differences.

6 Another tip for companies is to _____ as many local trade fairs and exhibitions as possible.

7 Mailshots are not advisable as the Chinese rarely _____ them.

8 Visitors should _____ the host's children as the family counts above all else in China.

3 Put the following words into the correct group.

an arrangement	a mailshot	business
conversation	a joint venture	an investment
a partnership	a request	research
a commitment	a relationship	preparatory work

make	do	enter into
an arrangement		

4 Look at the information comparing average prices in London and Beijing. Write a 120–140 word report comparing the cost of doing business in the two cities.

Index (London = 100) 0   50   100   150   200

Average cost of one night in a 5-star hotel

Average cost of office space per sq. metre

Average wage of a bilingual secretary

Average monthly rent for a small apartment

The cost of a 5-minute local phone call

5 Match the words as they appear in the unit.

1 generate   business cards
2 forge   sales
3 pledge   needs
4 produce   proceedings
5 swap   hospitality
6 provide   investment
7 start   trade literature
8 match   relationships

Articles

6 Complete the text by adding the necessary articles.

At meetings with Chinese, leader of your group will be expected to enter first and will generally be offered seat beside most senior Chinese person present. This person will usually chair meeting and act as host. At beginning of meeting, all people present will greet each other and swap business cards, after which period of small talk begins. Host will then officially start proceedings with brief introduction to Chinese enterprise. Visiting team is then invited to speak. It is appropriate at this point for foreign participants to make their case and answer questions. Following meeting Chinese enterprise will probably arrange special dinner for overseas guests along with other entertainment such as sightseeing. Guests should always accept these invitations as small talk in social setting is essential for forging relationships with Chinese.

Reading Test Part Three

- Read the following article on investing in shares and the questions on the opposite page.
- Each question has four suggested answers or ways of finishing the sentence, **A**, **B**, **C** and **D**.
- Mark **one** letter **A**, **B**, **C** or **D** for the answer you choose.

Investing in the stock market has always been more profitable than putting money into a traditional savings account. However, it is only in the last few years that private share ownership has become accepted as a reliable form of investment. There are many reasons why more and more people are now buying shares. To begin with, the whole process is now far more flexible and user-friendly and public awareness of investment products and their tax implications is a lot higher. Even more importantly, this awareness means people now realise that in the medium to long term shares are far more lucrative than deposit accounts. Today, people are also more likely to invest in a company for ethical reasons or as a show of support for that company.

When deciding to invest in shares, it is essential to think about your objectives. In order to avoid an expensive mistake, you need to consider your existing short and long-term financial commitments and how quickly you expect to see a return on your investment. Most importantly, you need to decide the extent to which you are prepared to speculate and then select the investment products which best reflect your attitude towards the perils inherent in any stock market investment.

At the end of the 1990s, newspapers were full of stories of investors realising massive profits, usually in connection with the flood of internet companies that issued shares over a short period of twelve months. Such companies, however, were anything but a safe investment. Although people were attracted by the phenomenal rate at which these companies were expanding, many investors saw their shares fall well below the issue price within months of buying them.

Private investors unwilling to tolerate high levels of risk can reduce uncertainty by buying shares in blue chip companies, which are established organisations such as banks or large international corporations. Although such an investment may minimise risk, it also limits the potential profits. Some investors try to remove the element of risk by closely monitoring stock market movements on a daily basis or by paying a regular sum into a managed fund over a long period of time. However, no matter how carefully people follow the markets or what expert advice they receive, statistics show that the safest option is to spread risk by investing in a wide range of different companies across different sectors.

As a first-time investor, it is vital to seek professional advice. Consultants can provide information on how to invest in the most attractive companies in both the UK and overseas. They can explain how stocks, shares, unit trusts and bonds actually work, how much each type of investment costs and, most importantly, which products best match their clients' requirements.

One reliable way of managing investments is through a broker, who charges a brokerage fee in the form of a percentage of the money invested. An alternative method is to deal in shares on the Internet. This incurs none of the regular broker's commission and investors can therefore easily afford to buy and sell shares more regularly. However, although some potential investors may find online trading exciting, they should be aware that direct trading is perhaps the least secure way of approaching the stock market, with few investors having the necessary skills and knowledge to make any profit whatsoever, never mind the fortunes popularised by the media.

1 According to the text, more people are now buying shares because

    A more ethical investments are available.

    B investors get a better rate of return.

    C investment periods are more flexible.

    D investors pay less tax on earnings.

2 What is the main consideration when deciding to invest in shares?

    A how much you pay for the shares

    B how quickly you can make a profit

    C how willing you are to take risks

    D how financially secure you are

3 Investors were attracted to internet companies because they

    A sold their shares at a low price.

    B had a large number of shares.

    C were often a very safe investment.

    D offered potential for rapid growth.

4 Investors can reduce risk and still make good profits by

    A investing only in blue chip companies.

    B monitoring share prices very closely.

    C buying shares gradually over time.

    D choosing a variety of investments.

5 What is the most useful advice for new investors?

    A the best time to invest in shares

    B the most suitable type of investment

    C the cheapest way to buy shares

    D the safest companies to invest in

6 Many investors buy and sell shares via the internet because it is

    A far cheaper.

    B much easier.

    C more exciting.

    D a lot safer.

Writing Test Part Two

- A friend of yours has applied for a new job which is similar to your current position. You have just received a letter asking you for a written reference.

- Write a **letter** of reference for your friend. Refer to relevant factors such as current responsibilities, personal qualities and suitability for the new position.

- Write **200–250** words.

The future of work

Visions

Reading 1   **1 Read the extract from a magazine article about the future of work and answer the questions.**

This is as good as it gets. The golden beach, the crystal clear water and the gentle refreshing breeze. You knew working from Sri Lanka for a few months would be a good idea, but this is paradise. Suddenly your pleasant thoughts are interrupted by your phone – the meeting, of course! Lying on the beach, you'd forgotten all about it. Quickly, you gather your things and head back to the rented beach house. You walk through the terrace doors and shout at your personal work organiser to download any mail and access all the meeting preparation files. On the wall a large flat monitor hums and flickers into life as you head into the shower. You walk back into the room to see your team leader's face on the wall giving details about the marketing project and today's objectives. You try to

pinpoint exactly what it is about him that you dislike, but you can't. Not that it matters, of course, because in six weeks the project will be over and you'll probably never see his face on your wall again. Your work organiser has already scanned the Web and applied for several new assignments. It knows what work you want to do and how much you expect to earn. It then does the rest for you – searching through the thousands of vacancies on the Web and selecting those most compatible with your CV, which, of course, it updates automatically before submitting. You forget the briefing for a moment and gaze out across the terrace at the waves gently lapping against the shore. Did people really use to work in the same office all their lives?

1   What year do you think the author is writing about?
2   What would be the advantages/disadvantages of this lifestyle?
3   Do you think this way of working will become reality?
4   Would you like to have this lifestyle?

Predictions

1 Five managers make predictions about the future of work. Look at the statements they make. Match each of the statements with one of the managers below.

1 People will work for more than one company at a time.
2 People will want to have more free time in the future.
3 There will be a lot more concern about health in the workplace.
4 As work becomes more flexible, people will work longer hours.
5 Governments will find it difficult to collect revenue from workers and companies.
6 Companies will have to ensure that communications remain polite.
7 Companies will be more closely involved with local communities.
8 Large organisations will become more powerful than some governments.

Jeanne Desaill – Director, MAS
In future, work space will become less rigid, with hotdesking being the norm. People will expect a better standard of working environment too. There's likely to be more shift work, partly to make better use of office equipment but also to offer services around the clock. In fact, I think working hours will probably change quite dramatically. For instance, there'll be no guarantee of free time even at the weekend. Some of the business community worry that staff won't work unless supervised but the real issue will be recognising when staff are overtaxing themselves.

Joshua Golder – Institute of Employment Studies
People are beginning to make the connection between lifestyle, performance and sickness, so I think we're bound to see a move towards promoting lifestyle issues in the office. The banning of smoking in public places is one example of this. There'll also undoubtedly be a lot of larger companies realising the importance of their social obligations. Smart firms are already pushing these responsibilities up the agenda and showing a lot more interest in the needs of people in their immediate environment.

Megan O'Riordan – Client Director, Dewbury Newton Carter
In future, part-time staff may be working for one employer in the morning and a different one in the afternoon, so values and branding will definitely need to be stronger. Staff interaction will be through telecommunications rather than the place of work. However, technology such as email has an impact on things like style and formality and old courtesies tend to disappear. So one requirement for a healthy organisation is certainly going to be maintaining respect in relationships.

Janice Watson – Staffordshire Teleworking Community
Companies will have to concentrate more on establishing employee loyalty, which will be hard won, with many people preferring to improve their CVs and move on to another company rather than get stressed out in their current job. Another issue is that with the growth in teleworking, how are authorities going to cope when all their taxation systems depend entirely on location? There's also no longer any clear distinction between employed and self-employed and, the way things are going, this distinction is set to disappear altogether.

Sachin Kapur – Director, Cyber Office
With people working from anywhere, there'll be a great change in employee demands in terms of contractual arrangements and the lifestyles of working people. They'll demand a healthier balance between work and leisure as it becomes less obvious when work 'stops'. What I'm worried about, however, is the erosion of people's rights if they're working for a huge company where there's little personal communication. And on a more global scale, how will a single state control a multinational which has far more resources and a lot more money?

Language

2 Look at the five texts again. How many different ways of expressing predictions can you find? Put the predictions in order of strength.

Speaking

3 Look at the eight statements on the previous page. Which of them do you agree with?

Reality

Listening

1 Cottice's Managing Director Neil Traynor talks about setting up a multi-occupant office building and his plans for the future. Listen and choose one letter for the correct answer.

1 Cottice Holdings' first office building was
  A a complex project.
  B occupied before completion.
  C a high risk project.

2 Cottice's intention was to
  A develop a place people would like.
  B create flexibility in the workplace.
  C share office space between friends.

3 How has the absence of hierarchy influenced the design?
  A All offices are the same size.
  B There are no reserved parking spaces.
  C People are allowed to socialise.

4 How does the building help tenants to network?
  A The lounge is a social area.
  B There are long corridors to walk down.
  C They are introduced in the reception area.

5 What encouraged Cottice to open the lounge?
  A Developments in technology enabled them to make changes.
  B The tenants asked for it.
  C The company realised it was necessary.

6 The picture gallery offers some benefits, such as
  A helping with identification of tenants, and with security.
  B helping staff on reception to recognise the tenants.
  C letting tenants know who is in the building.

7 How has the office community helped individuals work better?

A They can get away from the home environment.

B There are people to discuss ideas with.

C People are better motivated when they feel comfortable.

8 What has Cottice Holdings learned from its tenants?

A People like to socialise at work.

B This is a place where businesses can grow.

C Business is about making contacts.

Speaking

2 Work in pairs. Discuss the merits of each of these statements. How could they be changed to make them better reflect good working practices?

Your own work is your own responsibility. It's up to you how you do it. All that matters in the end is the result.

The best results come from a well motivated workforce. Any company must make motivation a priority if it is to achieve results.

There are right ways and wrong ways of doing things. The point of a corporate culture is to maximise the right ways and minimise the wrong. If you work here, you must work in the way managers decide.

Optional task

3 Use the internet to find out more about shared office space and write a 200–250 word summary on the pros and cons of office sharing.

e-business

What is e-business?

Speaking

1 What do you use the internet for at work? How has the way your business uses the internet changed over the past decade?

Reading

2 Look at The National B2B Centre's logo. What do you think this organisation does?

3 Read the information from The National B2B Centre's website. Write a brief definition for: e-business, e-trading, e-support, e-marketing.

4 What are the benefits of each?

The National B2B Centre
Helping growing businesses make smart e-business decisions

What is e-business?

E-business is the term used to describe the information systems and applications that support and drive business processes, most often using web technologies.

E-business allows companies to link their internal and external processes more efficiently and effectively, and to work more closely with suppliers and partners to better satisfy the needs and expectations of their customers, leading to improvements in overall business performance.

While a website is one of the most common implementations, e-business is much more than just a web presence. There is a vast array of internet technologies, all designed to help businesses work smarter, not harder.

Lots of solutions

Every business can benefit in some way from using e-business. Simple, low cost, or free technology is available to help you to:

- improve external product promotion and internal communication through effective e-marketing
- increase sales through effective deployment of e-commerce technologies
- streamline business processes with integrated back office systems
- reduce communication and travel costs using online meeting tools and shared workspaces
- maximise lead conversion by using CRM (Customer Relationship Management) systems to track and monitor interactions with prospects and clients
- improve supplier relations and productivity through collaborative tools and workspaces

E-commerce

Commerce has a long tradition of profiting from innovative systems and tools. As new technologies emerge, successful businesses are quick to identify developing opportunities and expand their commercial capabilities. Conducting commerce electronically (e-commerce or e-trading) is no different.

Electronic trading (e-trading) will support growth of your businesses' revenue by attracting new customers in new or traditional markets, by launching an online sales channel. It can deliver cost reductions by improving efficiency through automation and by creating a low-cost route to market for your products. Internet sales offer a higher margin than traditional routes. E-support uses online technologies to support your customers, at low cost, by providing information about your products and services on your website.

Trading online is not just about having a shopping cart and taking payments online. In order to fully realise the benefits, and save valuable resources, companies need to have effective sales processes on their websites and fully integrate them with robust back office systems.

E-marketing

The internet and related web technologies such as social networking are becoming more and more pervasive. While the basics of marketing remain unchanged (i.e. identifying and satisfying customer requirements profitably) businesses can now take advantage of better, more flexible and cheaper ways to market their goods and services to their target audiences.

The term e- (or online) marketing is, in simple terms, the use of the internet and related technologies to achieve marketing goals. E-marketing tends to revolve around a company's website, and combines other online marketing tools and techniques (such as direct email, search engines, online advertising and social networks) to acquire new customers and retain existing ones through the provision of online services.

Effectiveness

E-marketing does not stand alone, and to be truly effective it should be integrated with traditional marketing strategy and techniques. It does, however, bring a clear set of benefits, many of which are highly attractive to small and medium sized businesses:

- Costs can be considerably lower than for traditional marketing activity. This is partly because there is a greater ability for do-it-yourself activity, and partly because content can be reused very easily across different marketing channels (e.g. as website copy, an article or a blog). Online marketing isn't free, however, and prospective marketers need to recognise that paid-for, professional help may be essential.
- It is possible to reach a much wider audience (for a given budget) than for offline marketing, as geographic boundaries are removed. Passive tools such as websites or blogs can be found and accessed from most locations, while emails can be proactively sent to anybody whose address you have or purchase.
- Campaigns can be highly targeted and interactive. Pay-per-click advertising, for example, can be set up so that only specific keywords or phrases trigger an advert to be displayed in search results or on websites focusing on subjects related to your product or service. The upshot is an increase in response rates and an improvement in conversion ratios.

The advantages of e-business

 **1** Five managers talk about how Web technology has transformed an area of their business. Listen and decide which area and which benefit each speaker refers to.

Task one: area of business

Which area of business does each speaker say has been most transformed?

1 .....

2 .....

3 .....

4 .....

5 .....

A advertising methods

B after-sales service

C client information service

D customer purchasing process

E production processes

F supply management

G sales network

H training methods

Task two: benefit

Which is the main benefit each speaker mentions?

6 .....

7 .....

8 .....

9 .....

10 .....

I improved product support

J reduced operating costs

K increased turnover

L reduced staff turnover

M increased export activity

N reduced number of mistakes

O improved image

P reduced production times

Language

2 Look at the future perfect and future continuous forms in the following sentences. Could other verb forms be used? Find further examples of these forms in the audioscript and discuss how they are used.

*By the time the project's implemented, we'll **have networked** 300,000 employees.*
*And this year we'll **be delivering** up to 30 per cent of our courses by distance learning.*

Writing

3 Look at the graph showing the predicted growth of online and web-influenced retail sales.

Write a 120–140 word report comparing online retail sales and in-store sales influenced by websites with total retail sales.

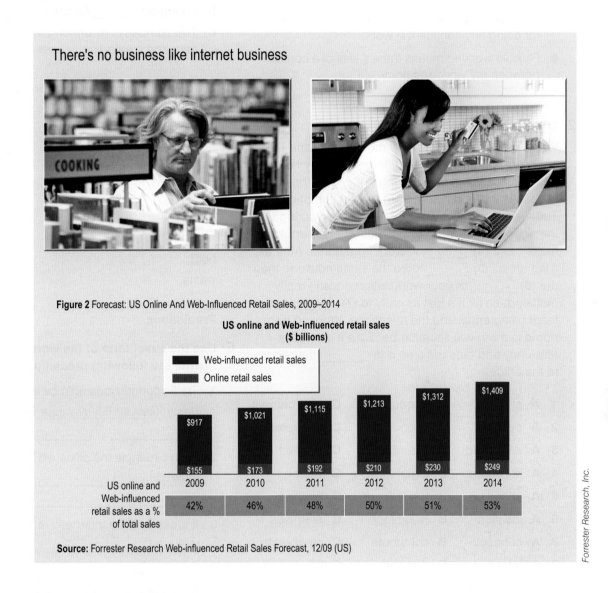

There's no business like internet business

Figure 2 Forecast: US Online And Web-Influenced Retail Sales, 2009–2014

US online and Web-influenced retail sales
($ billions)

- Web-influenced retail sales
- Online retail sales

	2009	2010	2011	2012	2013	2014
Web-influenced retail sales	$917	$1,021	$1,115	$1,213	$1,312	$1,409
Online retail sales	$155	$173	$192	$210	$230	$249
US online and Web-influenced retail sales as a % of total sales	42%	46%	48%	50%	51%	53%

Source: Forrester Research Web-influenced Retail Sales Forecast, 12/09 (US)

Forrester Research, Inc.

Optional task

5 Write a 200–250 word report on a company's website. Include information about the site's strengths and weaknesses and make recommendations for its further development.

1 Do the following statements refer to positive or negative situations at work?

1 He's been overtaxing himself a bit lately.

2 Our new line manager's really created a team spirit.

3 Some members of staff are struggling to cope with some of the new technology.

4 We have noticed that old courtesies have tended to disappear since we've been using email.

5 My new workstation makes it a bit more convenient for doing any confidential work.

6 Flexible working means there's less of a conflict between my work and home life.

2 Choose the correct word to fill each gap.

Well, I've been here for a few months now and I'm really enjoying it. It's quite different from my last job. For one thing, the working (1) _____ here is definitely very different from the old company. The managers have (2) _____ flexible working up the agenda and (3) _____ areas where it would make more (4) _____ to work from home. After all, if we are all (5) _____ onto the same network, then the (6) _____ of your workstation doesn't really matter, does it? It's just as easy to (7) _____ to a team using email and the telephone. Working from home is a win-win situation because it increases efficiency and cuts the time it (8) _____ travelling to the office.

1	A style	B surrounding	C environment
2	A pushed	B encouraged	C promoted
3	A controlled	B identified	C clarified
4	A sense	B logic	C value
5	A joined	B logged	C booked
6	A location	B workplace	C premises
7	A connect	B contribute	C co-operate
8	A lasts	B demands	C takes

3 Match the words.

1 book   premises

2 foster   a meeting room

3 key a number into   operations

4 run out of   a telephone terminal

5 show   team spirit

6 centralise   supplies

7 adapt to   interest

8 vacate   a new way of working

4 Complete each sentence with a suitable preposition.

1 There's a connection _____ lifestyle and performance in the workplace.

2 The use of email has a definite impact _____ things like formality in the office environment.

3 We're very dependent _____ the intranet, so if it goes down our operations are badly affected.

4 Some jobs, such as marketing, are more suited _____ flexible working than others.

5 I bumped _____ Sarah at the café this morning.

6 The company I'm working for now has even got a gym and a café _____ site.

5 Match the verbs with the appropriate nouns.

	a meeting	needs	time
save	✗	✗	✓
meet			
spend			
run			
predict			
suit			
hold			
waste			

Predictions

6 Use the exact form of the word in brackets to rewrite the following predictions.

1 Traffic congestion could be eased by teleworking.
(may) Teleworking may ease traffic congestion.
_____

2 I can't imagine the office will cease to be important.
(unlikely)
_____

3 It looks as if the internet's ready to explode.
(set)
_____

4 More people will want to work from home.
(bound)
_____

5 I don't think everyone will have an iPad®.
(improbable)
_____

6 Working from home is sure to increase in future.
(undoubtedly)
_____

Self-study 4b

1 Fill each gap with a suitable word.

Over the past decade more and more companies have developed the electronic sections of their business. Initially, they expected the internet to be **(1)** _____ more than an 'add on' to **(2)** _____ current business procedures. However, companies are now discovering **(3)** _____ electronic business will not just prove to be an efficient or cheaper sales channel **(4)** _____ will fundamentally change the way they do business. Companies in sectors **(5)** _____ as retailing or financial services are already realising substantial savings by using the internet to encourage **(6)** _____ growth of 'self-service' activities for customers and suppliers. Corporate intranets now allow staff to access training at **(7)** _____ time and make travel arrangements and file expenses online, reducing the costs **(8)** _____ are common to such processes.

2 Complete the puzzle. Which word runs vertically through the answers?

1 e-business is using _____ technology to transform basic business processes.

2 Most large companies now have a _____ where customers can access product information.

3 The internet is very flexible and allows companies to update their news _____ very quickly.

4 Many people worry about using credit cards to make financial _____ over the internet.

5 More and more people are getting connected to the internet and then buying goods _____ .

6 Many large companies have a secure company-wide computer network called an _____ .

7 The challenge is to _____ internet technologies into the company's business processes.

8 In order to access the World Wide Web, you need to use a web _____ .

9 Companies have to remember that e-business is about _____ and not technology.

3 Match the words as they appear in the unit.

1	take	offerings
2	manage	orders
3	improve	customer wants
4	handle	customer behaviour
5	communicate with	operating efficiencies
6	analyse	inventories
7	personalise	partners
8	anticipate	transactions

4 Match the words.

1	competitive	support
2	after-sales	advantage
3	product	turnover
4	staff	base
5	customer	learning
6	distance	service

Future perfect and future continuous

5 Use the prompts to write sentences using the future perfect and future continuous.

1 network / half our suppliers / by / end of this year
We'll have networked half our suppliers by the end of this year.

2 do / more online training / in future
_____
_____

3 not finish / report / by / end of next week
_____
_____

4 not use / any paper invoices / next year
_____
_____

5 complete / website / by July
_____
_____

6 rethink / internet strategy / over next few weeks
_____
_____

7 internet usage / double / within five years
_____
_____

8 not launch / products / until / website / complete
_____
_____

Listening Part One 🄠 2.01

- You will hear the Managing Director of a cosmetics manufacturer addressing a group of visitors about the history of the company.
- As you listen, for questions **1–12**, complete the notes using up to **three** words or a number.
- You will hear the recording twice.

The History of Eldertree Cosmetics

Early days

1 The company was established in _____ by Olivia Jenkins.

2 Her products sold well because of the _____ of natural products.

3 In order to satisfy demand, the owners had to find _____ in 1977.

The 1980s

4 The introduction of new products resulted in the _____ of the business.

5 By recruiting professional expertise, the company managed to secure _____ with major UK retailers.

6 To support further growth, Eldertree needed both the _____ of a bigger company.

7 In 1987 the company was acquired by Greenaway, the UK's largest _____ .

8 To improve productivity, Greenaway decided to build a _____ in 1988.

9 Greenaway also decided to keep Eldertree's _____ for its products.

Eldertree Cosmetics today

10 Greenaway has centralised functions such as its _____ .

11 In spite of its increased size, the company has kept a _____ .

12 In the last decade Eldertree has become a _____ both at home and abroad.

Part Two 🔘 (2.02)

- You will hear five different people talking about training courses.
- For each extract there are two tasks. For Task One, choose the course each speaker attended from the list **A–H**. For Task Two, choose the complaint each speaker makes about the course from the list **I–P**.
- You will hear the recording twice.

TASK ONE – TRAINING COURSE

- For questions **13–17**, match the extracts with the training course attended, listed **A–H**.
- For each extract, choose the training course attended.
- Write one letter **A–H** next to the number of the extract.

13   .....

14   .....

15   .....

16   .....

17   .....

A telephoning skills
B presentation skills
C time-management skills
D team-leadership skills
E assertiveness skills
F negotiating skills
G meeting skills
H writing skills

TASK TWO – COMPLAINT

- For questions **18–22**, match the extracts with the complaints, listed **I–P**.
- For each extract, choose the speaker's main complaint about the course.
- Write **one** letter **I–P** next to the number of the extract.

18   .....

19   .....

20   .....

21   .....

22   .....

I the course cost too much
J the food was disappointing
K the centre was too far away
L the course was too short
M the trainer was disorganised
N the course went on for too long
O the group was too big
P the course started late

Part Three 🎧 2.03

- You will hear an interview with the manager of a corporate travel agency.
- For each question **23–30**, mark **one** letter **A**, **B** or **C** for the correct answer.
- You will hear the recording twice.

23 The main effect of winning the award has been the increase in

   A staff motivation.

   B media publicity.

   C new business.

24 Why did Peter start *Corporate Direct*?

   A His local travel agencies had no vacancies.

   B His wife wanted him to work from home.

   C His ambition was to be self-employed.

25 Which *Corporate Direct* service is expanding most rapidly?

   A the car rental scheme

   B the company magazine

   C the currency exchange service

26 Why is *Corporate Direct* unique in the south-east?

   A It is an independent travel agency.

   B It holds detailed client information.

   C It offers the most competitive rates.

27 Which consultancy service is the most popular?

   A language training

   B travel insurance

   C business entertaining

28 Why do companies use a corporate travel agency?

   A It saves them valuable time.

   B It guarantees service standards.

   C It offers the best available prices.

29 *Corporate Direct*'s biggest clients are

   A financial service companies.

   B hotel and catering firms.

   C fashion retailers.

30 Which new service will be available to clients next?

   A an online reservation system

   B a new company credit card

   C a 24-hour telephone helpline

Reading Test Part Four

- Read the terms and conditions of employment below.
- Choose the best word to fill each gap.
- For each question **1–10**, mark **one** letter **A**, **B**, **C** or **D**.
- There is an example at the beginning (**0**).

Terms and Conditions of Employment

The employee works a 37$\frac{1}{2}$ hour week, which includes some evening work. The salary is based on Key Scale 3, with a (**0**) ..... for shift work. Weekday overtime is paid at a standard hourly (**1**) ..... , which increases to double-time at weekends. The employee's (**2**) ..... are as detailed in the attached letter of employment.

The salary is calculated from 25th–24th inclusive of each month and is (**3**) ..... to the employee's bank account on the last day of the month, except where the last day of the month falls on a weekend, in which case it is paid on the previous Friday.

The company's holiday year runs from April 1st each year. The employee is (**4**) ..... to two days' paid holiday per month worked, with three extra days' holiday during the Christmas period. All holidays must be taken within the holiday year (1st April–31st March). Those not taken by 31st March may not be (**5**) ..... over to the following year. All holiday dates are (**6**) ..... to management approval.

During the first four months of employment, the employee is on a period of (**7**) .... Within this period, employment may be (**8**) ..... by either party provided that at least one week's (**9**) ..... is given in writing.

The age of (**10**) ..... for all employees is 65. However, an employee may be allowed to work beyond this age, provided that the employment contract is renewed annually. The company does not operate a private pension scheme for employees.

Example

0   **A** bonus   **B** premium   **C** benefit   **D** prize

A	B	C	D
▬	☐	☐	☐

1 A charge	**B** rate	**C** fare	**D** tariff
2 A jobs	**B** routines	**C** duties	**D** tasks
3 A diverted	**B** accounted	**C** dispatched	**D** credited
4 A entitled	**B** authorised	**C** entrusted	**D** admitted
5 A passed	**B** taken	**C** carried	**D** put
6 A subject	**B** exposed	**C** subordinate	**D** referred
7 A appraisal	**B** placement	**C** analysis	**D** probation
8 A terminated	**B** destroyed	**C** eliminated	**D** abolished
9 A caution	**B** notice	**C** instruction	**D** advice
10 A removal	**B** release	**C** retirement	**D** resignation

The Reading Test

Overview

The Reading Test has six parts testing various reading skills. Part Four specifically tests a candidate's knowledge of vocabulary.

Part	Input	Task
1	Five 90 word texts	Matching sentences with texts
2	450–500 word text	Sentence level gap-filling
3	500–600 word text	Multiple-choice comprehension questions
4	250 word text	Single word multiple-choice gap-filling
5	250 word text	Single word gap-filling
6	150–200 word text	Proof-reading: identifying extra words

Length: 60 minutes

How to succeed

Here are some important general tips for doing the Reading Test.

- Read all instructions **carefully**.
- Begin with the part of the Reading Test you feel most confident about. You do not need to do the parts of the test in order.
- Leave difficult questions and return to them later if you have time.
- **Never** leave a question unanswered. If you run out of time or have no idea, guess.
- Leave enough time to do all the Writing Test. It represents 27 per cent of the final mark.
- Read through the whole text once before looking at the questions.
- The questions are generally in the same order as the answers. If you are confident that an answer is correct, begin reading for the next answer from that point, not from the beginning.
- Underline the answers in the text – it will make checking quicker.
- Only write one answer for each question.
- Use any time you have left to check your answers.

The reading tasks

1 **Part One tests the ability to read for both gist and specific information. Read the text and the three sentences below. Which sentence matches the text best? Underline the parts of the text which help you to identify the correct option.**

A   *Business Strategies for the Internet*

What opportunities does the internet offer your business? Can it make significant cost savings? Can it reshape your entire supply chain? *Business Strategies for the Internet* uses basic business principles to show how businesses can make best use of the internet. The authors argue that imagination and lateral thinking, not technical know-how, are the key sources of competitive advantage. They demonstrate why much corporate investment in the internet has been unsuccessful and show how failures could have been avoided. More than 100 case studies are analysed, showing how the internet's strengths have been successfully exploited. The authors are senior partners in *Net Gains*, one of the country's leading consultancies on the commercial exploitation of Web-based technology.

---

1   The authors demonstrate the importance of specialised technical skills.
2   The book shows how to cut distribution costs dramatically.
3   Real-life examples are used in the book to illustrate good practice.

Exam tips: Reading Test Part One

- The correct sentence will not normally use exactly the same words as the text.
- Words from the other, incorrect, sentences might appear in the text.
- Each text will normally be used at least once.
- Decide which is the best technique for you: reading each text first and then all the options, or reading each option first and then all five texts.

2 Part Two tests the ability to ensure that the overall meaning of a text is clear and that ideas are logically ordered and linked. Read the extract and the three sentences below. Which sentence fills the gap best? Why do the other sentences not fit?

are still faced by the question 'Will staff actually want to relocate?'.

To assume that staff will automatically relocate in order to keep their jobs is a mistake. They may have family commitments or regard the destination as undesirable. Staff that are being considered for relocation are probably valuable and could find another job locally. [**10**] This might not be cheap, but neither is losing key staff that the company has invested in over several years. The company needs to weigh up the attractiveness of

A It makes sense then to consult staff when choosing a destination for relocation.

B Therefore, a company needs to offer a package that will persuade them to move.

C By providing practical help, a company can minimise these difficulties.

Exam tips: Reading Test Part Two

- Read at least one sentence either side of each gap before filling it.
- Ensure that each sentence fits the gap grammatically.
- Pay special attention to linking words, reference words and pronouns.
- Check each sentence fits in with the logic of the text as a whole.
- Read the completed text to check your answers. Does it feel right?

3 Part Three tests the ability to read for specific information. Read the extract and the question below. Which option answers the question best?

Call centre technology has enabled companies to revolutionise their activities. Services such as freefone product information hotlines or the telephone-based distribution networks of companies like Direct Line Insurance are now cost-effective and easy to implement. Although sales may also be involved, with airlines, for example, using centralised reservations offices, call centres are not about telemarketing techniques such as cold calling consumers in the middle of their dinner to sell them double-glazing; they are a response to the fact that consumers now expect quick access to information when it suits them and not the company.

1 Why have call centres become so popular?
   A More and more people are buying products over the phone.
   B They are a cheap way for a company to distribute its goods.
   C People now expect fast and convenient customer service.
   D Freefone services are a successful marketing technique.

Exam tips: Reading Test Part Three

- Scan the text to find the relevant passage and read it carefully.
- Be careful of options that use the same words as in the text.
- Base all answers on information printed in the text – not world knowledge.
- Choose only one answer for each question.

Exam focus

4 Part Four tests vocabulary. Candidates complete a text by choosing one of four options to fill each gap. Before looking at the options on the next page, underline the words around each gap indicating the type of word missing. Think of a word for each gap.

Calgary Plastics has a policy of actively promoting the development of its staff. This is achieved in a range of ways throughout the company including induction courses, in-service training, training weekends, external training and appraisals.

We believe that this personal and professional development is of (**1**) ..... to both the company and individual employees. It enables the company to retain high-calibre, (**2**) ..... staff and thus offer a better product to our customers. It also provides us with a (**3**) ..... of able people with relevant experience for the management positions which inevitably (**4**) ..... within a large company such as Calgary Plastics.

Our focus on staff development and our policy of internal recruitment where possible mean that skilled employees have the opportunity to (**5**) ..... their careers rapidly within a framework which offers the necessary training to help them (**6**) ..... effectively in more senior positions.

This booklet is intended to assist us in (**7**) ..... your development by providing an easily accessible record of your training and professional development to date. It also (**8**) ..... appraisal procedures and gives advice on how to prepare for appraisal interviews.

Please try to ensure that you (**9**) ..... your records up to date and present your training portfolio at appraisal interviews so that your line manager or department head will be able to (**10**) ..... your future development needs.

Exam tips: Reading Test Part Four

- Read the whole text first to get a feel for the context and style.
- Use the words around each gap to predict the missing word.
- All the options are grammatically possible but only one is correct.
- Read the completed text to check your answers. Does it feel right?

5 Now choose the best word to fill each gap in the text on the previous page.

1	**A** profit	**B** credit	**C** benefit	**D** merit
2	**A** committed	**B** engaged	**C** contracted	**D** pledged
3	**A** fund	**B** pool	**C** collection	**D** store
4	**A** present	**B** arise	**C** happen	**D** develop
5	**A** progress	**B** elevate	**C** advance	**D** raise
6	**A** function	**B** serve	**C** practise	**D** officiate
7	**A** proving	**B** testing	**C** controlling	**D** monitoring
8	**A** outlines	**B** portrays	**C** represents	**D** displays
9	**A** maintain	**B** keep	**C** retain	**D** hold
10	**A** guess	**B** value	**C** assess	**D** rate

6 Part Five tests grammar and understanding of cohesion. Candidates complete a gapped text with suitable words. No options are given. Underline the words around each gap which help you identify the missing word. Now fill the gaps.

Female entrepreneurs as successful as men

A report published this week by WestLink Small Business Services shows that women are still (**1**) ..... likely to start new business ventures than men, although they are usually better qualified and more realistic in their business planning. The report found (**2**) ..... women were responsible for roughly 27 per cent of the self-employment market in the UK and that this percentage has not changed since the early 1990s. Moreover, there has been little change in the proportion of male to female start-ups over the years (**3**) ..... the growth in women-owned businesses in areas such as nannying, fitness training, gardening and interior design.

Few banks are addressing this issue. A WestLink spokesman, (**4**) ....., would like to see more women starting their own business ventures: 'Studies have shown that gender has (**5**) ..... effect whatsoever on the potential success of a business. The crucial factors are age, vocational qualifications, amount of relevant experience and the number of people employed by the start-up business.'

Most businesses started by women tend to be in certain industries (**6**) ..... as domestic and professional services, catering and leisure. This might be explained by the fact that these areas typically offer more flexible working patterns, (**7**) ..... is a major factor for working women with families.

One distinct difference (**8**) ..... male and female entrepreneurs concerns the level of first year turnover predicted in their business plans. Men, on average, forecast a first year turnover of £150,000 (**9**) ..... women hoped to make a more modest £74,000 on their first year's trading. The report showed that the lower figure represented a more realistic approach (**10**) ..... than lower expectations.

Exam tips: Reading Test Part Five

- Read the whole text first to get a feel for the context and style.
- Read at least one sentence either side of each gap before filling it.
- Fill each gap with only one word.
- Read the completed text to check the grammar is correct. Is the overall meaning clear?

7 Part Six tests proof-reading ability. Candidates identify any extra words in the numbered lines of a short text. Some lines are correct. Read the following text and underline the incorrect words. Why are they incorrect?

Language skills in business

0	In today's global markets, businesses have to communicate internationally
00	and every language barriers have to be overcome. That's the reason why
1	people with good language skills they are needed by international
2	businesses order to negotiate with customers, deal with suppliers,
3	contribute to meetings and manage overseas subsidiaries. One of the best
4	ways to deal with such a varied language needs is through well-planned and
5	relevant language learning programmes. An individual training programme
6	which can focus on the precise language skills people need to do their job
7	properly and help them to achieve their learning objectives appropriately.
8	Developing language skills takes time but the effective communication is
9	crucial in today's international markets.

Exam tips: Reading Test Part Six

- Read the whole text first to get a feel for the context and style.
- Underline any words which seem strange.
- Concentrate on small grammatical words such as articles, pronouns and prepositions.
- Make sure you have no more than one mistake on any single line.
- Read the whole sentence to check whether your answer is correct.
- Read the completed text to check your answers. Does it feel right?

The Listening Test

Overview

The Listening Test has three parts.

Part	Input	Task
1	3–4 minute monologue	Gap-filling (words and numbers)
2	Five short monologues	Matching monologues with topics/places etc. Matching the same monologues with functions, attitudes, opinions etc.
3	4–5 minute conversation	Multiple-choice comprehension questions

Length: A total of 15 minutes of listening material played twice, plus 10 minutes at the end to transfer answers to the Answer Sheet.

Before listening

It is important that you use your time well before you listen. Here are some tips.

- Read the instructions **very carefully** before you listen.
- Check the type of answer you need to give.
- You will always be given time to read through the questions before you listen. Use this time well. Try to predict what you might hear and what the answers might be.

1 **Look at the following form from Part One of a Listening Test. Predict words that might fill the gaps and complete the notes.**

PART ONE

- You will hear a company representative outlining the programme of a sales conference.
- As you listen, for questions **1–12**, complete the notes using up to **three** words or a number.
- You will hear the recording twice.

Annual Sales Conference

The programme

1 9.30   The conference will begin with .... in the main foyer.

2 10.00   This will be followed by a report on .... by Nigel Laws, Group MD.

3 11.30   There will be a short break for .... before the first workshop.

While listening

1 Look at the following Part Three question and the audioscript below. Why might some candidates choose a wrong option?

2 The company dramatically improved its profits by
   A cutting production costs.
   B developing new products.
   C reducing product prices.

> **Exam tip:**
> Always listen carefully to the whole recording. Incorrect options often use the same words that you hear.

	...needed to improve margins.
Interviewer	So just how did you manage to improve profits so dramatically?
Annette	Well, first of all, we looked at ways of cutting production costs and the possibility of a large advertising campaign to re-launch existing brands. But in the end we decided to revamp our lines - several people at the time wanted to win market share back by aggressive discounting but we were confident that our designers could win back customers with fresh, exciting ideas. It meant a lot of investment, but it's paid off.
	It certainly has. What in...

After listening

1 Always check your answers very carefully. Look at the question papers below. Find the candidate's mistakes.

PART ONE
- You will hear a PR Manager talking about a forthcoming press launch.
- As you listen, for questions **1–12**, complete the notes using up to **three** words or a number.
- You will hear the recording twice.

XR300 Press Launch

The programme

1 9.30   Welcome speech by Tom Watts, ...*Who is the Director*.... of Axon UK.

PART TWO: TASK ONE
- You will hear five different people talking about their jobs.
- For each extract there are two tasks. For Task One, choose the job title of each speaker from the list **A–H**.
- You will hear the recording twice.

13 ...*A/B*...
14 ...*A*...

A Secretary
B Accountant
C Receptionist

PART THREE
- You will hear an interview with the manager of a large retailer.
- For each question **23–30**, mark one letter **A**, **B** or **C** for the correct answer.
- You will hear the recording twice.

23 The company is looking to expand in order to
   Ⓐ increase its profit margins.
   B extend its range of products.
   Ⓒ break into foreign markets.

The Writing Test

Overview

The Writing Test has two parts.

Part	Input	Task
1	Instructions and graph	Writing a short description of a graph (120–140 words)
2	Instructions	Writing a letter, short report or proposal (200–250 words)
	Length: 70 minutes	

How to succeed

The Writing Test assesses performance in several areas: task completion, organisation and linking of ideas, appropriateness, range and accuracy of vocabulary and grammar.

Task

- Successful task completion means fulfilling all parts of the task. Full marks can be awarded only when all the points in the rubric are covered fully and appropriately.
- Keep to the word limit. If you are below it, you have probably not fully completed the task. If you are above it, you have probably included unnecessary information.

Language

- Show a range of grammar and vocabulary.
- Organise and link your ideas clearly.
- Use language which is consistent and appropriate.
- Check your writing **carefully** when you have finished.

Describing graphs

1 **Part One tests the ability to describe a graph. Look at the following task and the sample answer below. Does the answer fulfil the task?**

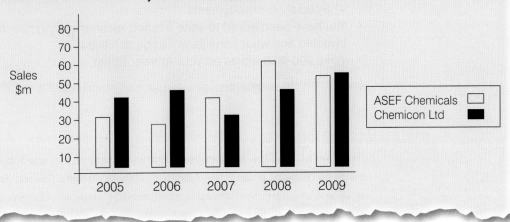

PART ONE
- The graph below shows sales for two companies between 2005–2009.
- Using information from the graph, write a short **report** describing and comparing the performance of the two companies during this period.
- Write **120–140** words on your Answer Sheet.

Exam tip:
You have little time and only a few words, so describe general trends. Don't just give a long list of detailed, individual movements.

In 2005 ASEF Chemicals made sales of just a little bit over $30m and then in the following year, which was 2006, the sales at ASEF Chemicals went down to about the $25m level. The next year, however, sales went up very quickly and ASEF Chemicals made slightly over $40m but the next year sales went up even more quickly than they did the year before and they reached $60m in 2008. But then, in 2009, the sales dropped just a little bit and ASEF Chemicals made sales of about only $50m, which wasn't very good for that company.

Sales at Chemicon Ltd started higher at over $40m, which was about $10m more than at ASEF Chemicals but they only went up a little bit the following year to about the $45m level. But then sales at Chemicon Ltd fell very much and were only at $30m, which was a lot less than ASEF Chemicals. But in both the next year, which was 2008, and in 2009 they went back up again and the sales achieved a bit over $50m by the end of 2009, which was just a little bit more than ASEF Chemicals.

2 **Consider how the following affect the conciseness of the sample answer.**

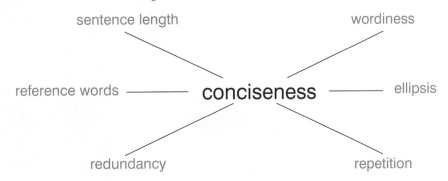

How else can the sample answer be improved? Rewrite it in 120–140 words.

Report writing

1 In Part Two candidates may be asked to write a short report. Read the following task and the sample answer below. Does the answer fulfil the task?

PART TWO

- Your company has decided to invest some of this year's exceptionally high profits in one of the following areas:
  - New computers
  - Language training courses
  - Special bonus payments.
- You have been asked to write a report recommending how the profits should be invested and what benefits would be achieved.
- Write **200–250** words on your Answer Sheet.

This report is about how the company should invest some of this year's exceptionally high profits into one of the following areas – New Computers, Language Training Courses, Special Bonus Payments. First of all new computers. Most employees have computers which are fast enough to handle the work which they normally do on them. These computers are not very old. The company wants to increase its export sales. This is especially in Spain and France. Language training courses would be a very good idea for all the staff who have to speak with business partners and customers in these countries.

The staff would enjoy the lessons and feel that the company is investing in them. Moreover, it is good for motivation. Furthermore, special bonus is also good for motivation however does not invest anything in the company. The staff might expect to get such bonus every time the company makes good profits and then there might be some problems. It is not recommended. Finally, who do you give the special bonus to? It can cause problems. I think it would be the best if the company invests the high profits in language training because that is the best for both the staff and the company. The courses should be for anyone who has contact with partners and customers.

2 **What main points do you think the writer is trying to make? What reasons does he/she give in support of these main points?**

Main points	Supporting ideas

3 **Is the sample answer organised in logical paragraphs? How many paragraphs does the report need?**

4 **Rewrite the sample answer to make the writer's original ideas easier to understand. Consider the following.**

paragraphing   layout (headings, bullets etc.)

organisation of reports

main points and supporting ideas   linking words and phrases

5 **Look at the Writing Test Assessment Sheet on page 78. Consider the questions and make any necessary changes to your report.**

Formal letter writing

1 Alternatively, candidates may be asked to write a formal letter in Part Two. Read the following task and a candidate's handwritten notes below.

PART TWO

- A foreign business associate is visiting your company for three days. You have been asked to organise the visit and plan appropriate entertainment.
- Write a letter to the visitor outlining a timetable for the visit and describing the activities you have planned.
- Write **200–250** words on your Answer Sheet.

Thursday
Pick Ricardo up at 10.15 from the airport
Take him to hotel and check in
Business lunch & then to company for meeting
Dinner at Ricardo's hotel – time to be arranged

Friday
Meeting at company 9.30
Working lunch – get sandwiches delivered
Meeting until about 17.00
Give Ricardo time to freshen up
Dinner at The Riverside Lodge restaurant 20.00

Saturday
Ricardo in company golf tournament – tee off at 8.30
Formal dinner with speaker at golf club 19.30

Sunday
Return flight to Madrid 09.45

Now use the candidate's notes to write the letter. Consider the following.

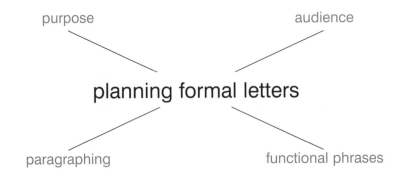

purpose   audience

planning formal letters

paragraphing   functional phrases

2 Look at the Writing Test Assessment Sheet on page 78. Consider the questions and make any necessary changes to your letter.

Essential report writing phrases

Introduction
This report aims/sets out to ...
The aim/purpose of this report is to ...
The report is based on ...

Findings
It was found that ...
The following points summarise our key findings.
The key findings are outlined below.

Conclusion (s)
It was decided/agreed/felt that ...
It is clear that ...
No conclusions were reached regarding ...

Recommendation (s)
It is suggested/proposed/recommended that
We (strongly) recommend that ...
It is essential to ...
It would be advisable to ...

Signalling
The following areas of concern have been highlighted.
There are a number of reasons for ...
There are several factors which affect ...
A further factor is ...
This raises a number of issues.
As might have been expected, ...
Contrary to expectations, ...

Essential letter writing phrases

Referring to previous contact
Thank you for your interest ...
With reference to your letter of/dated ... in which ...
Further to our conversation of ...

Stating the reason for writing
I am writing to confirm/apply for/outline ...
I would like to thank/complain/comment on ...
I am writing concerning ...

Enclosing information
Please find enclosed ...
As requested, I enclose ...

Offering assistance
Should you have any further questions, please contact me on the above number.
In the meantime, if you require any further information, please do not hesitate to call me.

Referring to future contact
I look forward to hearing from you/meeting you/seeing you/working with you.
I hope to hear from you soon.

Writing Test Assessment Sheet

TASK	Are all the points in the rubric adequately covered?	
	Is the answer the correct length?	
ORGANISATION	Is it easy to follow the writer's ideas?	
	Are the writer's main points adequately supported?	
	Is the layout clear and appropriate? (paragraphs, headings, bullets etc.)	
CLARITY	Is the answer free of redundancy and repetition?	
	Are the sentences of an appropriate length?	
	Are linking words and phrases used clearly and naturally?	
LANGUAGE	Is there a range of vocabulary, grammar and functional language?	
	Is the language generally accurate?	
	Is the formality and tone appropriate and consistent?	
COMMENTS		

The Speaking Test

Overview

The Speaking Test takes place with two, or possibly three, candidates and two examiners. The first examiner speaks to the candidates. The second examiner listens and assesses the candidates' English.

Part	Format	Input	Task
1	Examiner talks to each candidate individually	Examiner asks questions	Speaking about yourself Responding to questions
2	Candidate talks to candidate	Written prompt	Giving a one-minute talk
3	Candidates discuss a topic together	Written prompt	Completing a collaborative task

How to succeed

The Speaking Test assesses performance in a number of areas. Here are some important tips for each area.

Interactive communication

• Listen **carefully** to all instructions.

• Ask the examiner to repeat any instructions you are not sure about.

• Give full appropriate answers, not just one or two words.

• Keep to and complete the task. Do not talk about other things.

• Good communication means working with and not competing with the other candidate.

Organisation of ideas
Consider the following:

• your main points

• your supporting ideas

• how to order and link your ideas.

Grammar and vocabulary

• You will be marked on both the range and accuracy of your grammar and vocabulary. You therefore need to demonstrate variety in your language. However, if you try to be too ambitious, you risk being penalised for lack of accuracy.

Pronunciation

• Speak clearly and at a natural speed.

Personal information

1 In Part One of the Speaking Test the examiner will ask the candidates some general questions about themselves. Work in pairs. Your teacher will give you some cards. Take a card and ask your partner about the topic on the card.

Candidate 1   Candidate 2

Examiner 1

Examiner 2

Exam tips: Speaking Test Part One

- Ask the examiner to clarify if you do not fully understand a question.
- Answer each question fully and keep to the question.
- Speak to the examiner and not the other candidate in Part One.
- Do not interrupt the other candidate in this part of the test.

Short talk

1 In Part Two of the Speaking Test each candidate talks for one minute on one of three given topics. Candidates are given a minute to prepare their ideas. Look at the following topics. Which would you choose to talk about? Why?

Business Travel:	The importance of a good hotel when travelling on business
Sales:	How to provide good customer service
Marketing:	The importance of good product positioning

2 Listen to Natacha and Salvatore giving their talks. Use the Speaking Test Assessment Sheet on page 83 to assess their performance.

2.04

Exam focus

3 Now listen to Natacha and Salvatore doing the task again. In what way is their performance better?

(2.05)

4 Following each short talk, the other candidate is expected to ask a relevant question. What questions would you ask Natacha and Salvatore?

5 Use the framework below to plan a one-minute talk on one of the following topics.

Communication:	How to ensure good communication within teams
Personnel:	The importance of providing staff training
Finance:	How to raise capital for new investment

Exam tip:
Use your preparation time well. List and order your main points and supporting ideas.

Opening sentence: _____
_____

Main points

- _____
- _____
- _____

Supporting ideas

- _____
- _____
- _____

Concluding sentence: _____
_____

6 Now work in pairs. Take turns to give your talk. Use the Speaking Test Assessment Sheet on page 83 to assess your partner's performance.

Exam focus

Collaborative task

1 Part Three tests the ability to discuss a given issue and reach certain decisions. Look at the following task and the Speaking Test Assessment Sheet on the opposite page. Then listen to Natacha and Salvatore and assess their performance.

> Your company is entertaining foreign visitors for three days. You have been asked to organise social activities for them. Discuss and decide together:
> - which company representatives the guests should meet
> - what activities would be suitable.

Exam tips: Speaking Test Part Three

- Read the task instructions very carefully.
- Use the preparation time given to organise your ideas.
- Begin by quickly agreeing on a context (the type of company you work for etc.).
- Give reasons to support your ideas.
- Invite your partner to express his/her ideas and respond to them.
- When you disagree, say why and give an alternative idea.
- Make sure you are moving the task towards a conclusion.
- Recap and summarise your decisions when necessary.

2 Now listen to Natacha and Salvatore doing the same task again. In what way is their performance better?

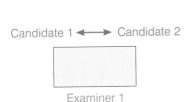

Candidate 1 ⟷ Candidate 2

Examiner 1

Examiner 2

3 Work in pairs. Do the following task.

> Your company is launching a new product. You have been asked to organise a public relations event as part of the launch. Discuss and decide together:
> - who should be invited
> - what the programme should involve.

Speaking Test Assessment Sheet

		Student A	Student B
SHORT TALK	Does the student show a clear understanding of the task?		
	Is there an appropriate introduction and conclusion?		
	Are the student's ideas well-organised and logically ordered?		
	Is appropriate signposting and linking language used?		
	Does the student develop ideas rather than repeat them?		
	Are the ideas clearly expressed and easy to understand?		
	Does the student speak in a clear and natural manner?		
	Is the talk of an appropriate length?		

COMMENTS

		Student A	Student B
COLLABORATIVE TASK	Does the student show a clear understanding of the task?		
	Is there an attempt to establish a shared context?		
	Does the student give reasons to support opinions?		
	Does the student listen and respond to other opinions?		
	Are the student's ideas easy to understand?		
	Does the student ask for clarification when necessary?		
	Does the student agree and disagree appropriately and naturally?		
	Does the student summarise and move the task towards a conclusion?		

COMMENTS

Staff motivation

What motivates staff?

Speaking

1 Read the following statements. Do you agree? Why/Why not?

- Managers assume that the goals of employees are those of the company.
- Motivation stems from job satisfaction and not financial reward.

Money

Time

Holiday

Facilities

Business Travel

Company Car

Look at these suggestions for motivating staff. Rank them in order of importance. Give reasons for your answers.

Reading

2 Read the newspaper article on the opposite page. What is the writer's attitude to motivational techniques? Do you share this attitude?

Meeting the company's motivational challenge

Adrian Furnham discusses the thorny issue of putting motivational techniques into practice.

[handwritten: Do you know any?]

Managers, company owners and supervisors have always been frustrated and bewildered by employees with little or no motivation. We have all seen the 'quit-but-stay' employees who have severed their psychological contact with the organisation. Nothing seems to fire them up. They firmly park their brains and their enthusiasm for life in the staff car park in the morning, re-engaging them with gusto 30 seconds after the official end of work time.

[handwritten: How does this make you feel?]

However, they shrewdly avoid doing anything that warrants dismissal and are content to keep their heads down, doing the minimum and volunteering nothing. This leaves the company with little option other than to mark them down as candidates for the next round of redundancies.

But what management techniques are available to repair and restore motivation?

❑ *Give employees as much meaningful work as possible. The less intrinsically interesting the work, the more needs to be done to make it acceptable: job enrichment, job rotation and job sharing.*

❑ *Give employees the information and resources needed to do a good job. Also ensure, through ongoing training, that employees have the necessary skills to meet the requirements of the job.*

❑ *Demonstrate a commitment to career development and promotion from within.*

❑ *Foster a sense of team spirit. You do not have to organise outdoor assault courses. It is enough to provide opportunities for people to meet, talk and share together.*

[handwritten: Which techniques do you think are more effective?]

❑ *Publicly recognise and congratulate employees for good work. Celebrate success; create heroes.*

❑ *Provide regular and specific feedback to all staff through both formal appraisals and informal channels of communication. Encourage feedback from staff and involve employees in decisions that affect their work.*

❑ *Pay people what they are worth. Consider such factors as market forces, predatory competitors and the contribution each individual makes.*

The astute reader may be tempted to ask: so what is really new? The answer is: nothing really.

[handwritten: What's popular today?]

Ideas in motivation get repackaged, renamed and rebranded, but fundamentally remain the same as ever. Fads and fashions in the management consultancy world seem to dictate which particular technique is seen as the most powerful and popular at any given time.

The fact that we know some of the key factors in motivation, however, has not prevented many managers from ignoring them. Some people are fortunate enough to have a good boss, who may have modelled positive motivational behaviours. But because few managers are trained or educated in the art of motivation and have themselves never been well-managed, we get the perpetuation of incompetence.

[handwritten: Do you know any such bosses?]

This explains the paradox of why people have heard about but not seen successful motivational management in practice.

Adapted from the *Sunday Telegraph*

Speaking   **3** **Read the article again and discuss the handwritten questions.**

A motivation survey

 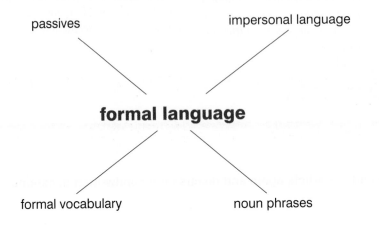

1 Terrain Ltd, a leisurewear manufacturer, is investigating staff motivation. Listen to five employees talking to the HR Manager. Which grievance does each speaker refer to?

1 .....
2 .....
3 .....
4 .....
5 .....

A too much responsibility
B uninteresting work
C lack of communication
D uncooperative colleagues
E lack of recognition
F unsatisfactory pay
G inflexible working hours
H lack of clear objectives

Language

2 Look at the HR Manager's incomplete report on staff motivation on the opposite page. Underline examples of the following features.

passives   impersonal language

formal language

formal vocabulary   noun phrases

3 Complete the *Findings* section of the report by summarising the grievances of the Terrain employees.

Report on Staff Motivation

Introduction
This report presents the results of the recent survey of staff motivation. The findings are based on interviews with employees from all departments within the company.

Findings

Conclusion
It is clear that there are significant levels of dissatisfaction regarding certain issues within the company. Unless these issues are addressed as a matter of urgency, the consequent demotivation of staff will undoubtedly have a negative impact on the performance of the company.

Recommendations

➡Ellough Industrial Estate ➤ BECCLES ➡ Suffolk ❀ NR34 7RY ✒ Tel 01502 714281 ✦ Fax 01502 714282 ❀

4 What recommendations would you make to address the grievances? Use your ideas to complete the report.

5 Design a questionnaire to find what motivates your fellow students in English lessons.

Recruitment

Recruitment methods

Speaking

1 What are the advantages and disadvantages of the following?

- internal recruitment
- job advertisements
- recruitment agencies
- headhunting

...d was keen to install a candidate for the new position as a delay in

..l be headed by ... Stevens, who will lead the new Finance Division of the company.

...ccept-corporations. ...with the new ...e in place it ...s unlikely that the CEO will be capa-of maintaining such ...trict control over the company's recruitment policy, which, up until now, has dictated the type of candidates that

HEAD HUNTERS plc

So · How did you get on with your first day in the field?

Cartoon by Colin Wheeler

Reading

2 Read the first two paragraphs of the article on the facing page. Match the sentences in italics with the following functions.

explaining	comparing	emphasising	contrasting	exemplifying

3 Now complete the article by choosing the best sentence to fill each gap.

A They are the currency by which headhunting operates.

B If, for example, the original contact is unavailable, a colleague will answer the phone and happily divulge their own name.

C All of these conversations with the headhunter will be handled discreetly to save any embarrassment at work.

D A team of researchers will have done some initial searching and compiled a list of suitable candidates.

E With clever questioning, the headhunter can navigate around the rest of the department and quickly compile a list of names and likely job roles.

F Anyone contributing to an online newsgroup with informed, specialist opinion may well become the target of a headhunter.

So why do people headhunt?

'The reason headhunting works is because we target the individual,' says Adelaide Macaulay of London-based Morgan Howard International. 'If a company needs to fill a niche role in a niche market, then they'll come to us.' Macaulay recruits for a number of clients spread throughout Europe. Each company needs to fill an important or highly-specialised role and thinks traditional advertising would not be effective. *This is particularly the case as 99 per cent of the people Macaulay targets are not actively on the market.* She usually targets people who are happy in their job and not looking to move. However, an Achilles heel can usually be found that allows the headhunter to persuade them that they are, in fact, wanting to change. *It may be that they are fed up with the company, that they want more money, or that they want a change of location.*

Internet headhunting firm Netsearch is more blunt than Macaulay about the reason why companies turn to headhunters: 'Headhunting is relatively cheap and on the increase as selection gets worse and worse.' Recruiters divide their business into 'selection' and 'search' processes. *The former category refers to traditional advertising and the latter to the activities of the headhunter.* Recruitment officers believe that for certain vacancies advertising is too expensive and throws up hundreds of largely unsuitable CVs, which take hours to process. *Headhunters, on the other hand, have enough tricks up their sleeve to produce a shorter, better quality list of candidates.* With Netsearch, they insist, you can get a better person more quickly.

Headhunters are understandably unwilling to reveal their methods. However, one source did claim that if he had one name and extension number, within a matter of hours he would have a good idea of who everyone in the department is and what they do. 1 By a simple process of deduction, it is then easy to work out that person's position in the company; if people are sitting at adjacent desks, the chances are that they are in similar roles. 2 This information can then be stored for future reference.

One thing all of this makes clear is the importance of names. 3 Any name a headhunter comes across is written down and put on record. This process has been made much easier with the invention of email, which indicates a person's name, employer and even the department they work in. 4 Companies like Netsearch constantly monitor such forums hunting for potential candidates.

Adapted from the *www.taps.com* website

4 **Underline the reference words and phrases in the text. Which refer to a passage of text and not to a single noun?**

Speaking

5 **A key staff member has just left your company and you have been asked to recruit a replacement. Discuss and decide the following.**

- the qualities required for the job
- the best method of recruiting a replacement

The headhunting process

1 Dave Archer specialises in executive search in the IT sector. Listen to his presentation about headhunting and complete the notes using up to three words or a number.

Headhunting

A presentation by Dave Archer from the executive search firm ArcherGoodall Associates

- **Introduction**

1 The UK recruitment market is divided into four categories: _____ , advertising selection, a combination of the two and executive search.

2 The headhunting market is expanding due to _____ within specific markets, especially in the finance, consulting and information technology sectors.

- **The headhunting process**

3 The headhunter begins by identifying possible candidates through _____ or extensive contact networks.

4 After making contact, the headhunter interviews candidates at their company offices or at a _____ .

5 The headhunter then collates candidates' CVs and _____ to the client, who shortlists three or four candidates.

6 The client then interviews the candidates, after which the headhunter provides feedback and assists in the _____ to ensure a successful conclusion.

- **Fees**

7 The headhunter will charge a percentage of the appointee's _____ .

8 The fee is normally charged as _____ , a shortlist fee and a completion fee.

- **The advantages of headhunting**

9 Headhunters offer knowledge of the market, their client's business, their _____ and those of their competitors.

10 This is achieved through extensive research, contact with the _____ in the market and international exposure.

11 Headhunting saves clients time and gives them access to _____ information.

12 Headhunting identifies people who are professionally satisfied, _____ and highly competent – exactly the type of people who can most benefit the client.

2 Look at the following checklist for planning short talks. Listen to Dave's presentation again. How does he address the following points?

Don't forget

Planning short talks

Remember these points when planning a short talk.

- **Purpose**
  What is the purpose of the talk? (e.g. to explain a procedure)

- **Content**
  What are the main points?
  How are these points supported?

- **Organisation**
  How could you order your main points?
  (e.g. chronological sequence)
  How could you introduce and conclude your talk?

- **Language**
  What linking words and phrases could you use?
  What other useful phrases could you use?

Speaking
1.23–1.24

3 Talk about one of the following topics for one minute. Prepare your talk using the questions above.

- how to fill a key vacancy
- the importance of having a good CV

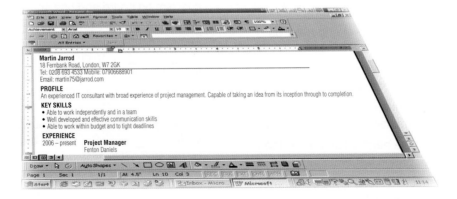

Writing

4 Find a job advertisement and write a 200–250 word letter of application. Include your reasons for applying and explain what you can bring to the job.

Self-study 5a

1 Some of the following lines contain an unnecessary word. Underline any extra words in lines 1–14.

1 The findings are being based on interviews with ten
2 senior managers and two directors which as well as
3 a questionnaire sent to more than fifty employees
4 at the leisurewear manufacturer's main production
5 facility in Suffolk. It was found that such levels of
6 staff motivation were extremely low throughout
7 of the organisation. In particular, staff expressed
8 any dissatisfaction with their current salary levels
9 and said they felt undervalued by the company. It
10 was also found that those inflexible working hours
11 are a certain major grievance among staff at all
12 levels. Other reasons given for job dissatisfaction
13 included uncooperative colleagues, lack of the clear
14 objectives and too much responsibility.

2 Add un, in or ir to each of the following words to form its opposite.

1 effective _____
2 significant _____
3 satisfactory _____
4 regular _____
5 appreciated _____
6 flexible _____
7 responsible _____
8 interesting _____
9 capable _____
10 specific _____

Now use either form of the words to complete the following sentences.

1 We pay competitive salaries because we don't want our people to feel _____ and undervalued.

2 Some managers are _____ of understanding that an employee's goals might not be the company's.

3 You can motivate workers by ensuring that they always have _____ and varied work.

4 I find it a lot easier when I'm working towards _____ objectives and goals.

5 Progress meetings tend to be spontaneous and held at pretty _____ intervals.

6 Any motivational technique will be _____ if the employees are determined not to enjoy their work.

7 All the way through the negotiations both sides remained _____ on the issue of longer hours.

8 Management dismissed the union's behaviour as _____ and unreasonable.

3 Match the verbs with a similar meaning. Then think of a word or phrase to follow each verb.

1 remain —————— cut
2 restore —————— stay
3 schedule   resign
4 appreciate   deal with
5 sever   rebrand
6 rename   repair
7 address   value
8 quit   plan

4 Complete each sentence with a suitable preposition.

1 I prefer working on big projects because I like to have something to get my teeth _____ .

2 A lot of the problem stems _____ a personality clash between Helen and her line manager.

3 Attitudes _____ motivational techniques vary substantially within the workforce.

4 In terms of pay and conditions, I don't think we are falling _____ our competitors.

5 There's a lack _____ promotion opportunities.

6 Not working overtime is often seen _____ a failure to show commitment to the company.

Passives

5 Complete the text. Put each verb in brackets into the correct form of the passive.

In order to assess past performance and review pay, all employees (1 *appraise*) _are appraised_ at least once a year. Pay increases (2 *award*) _____ on the basis of performance and (3 *not/base*) _____ on the length of service at the company. Despite the fact that this system (4 *criticise*) _____ by employees ever since it (5 *introduce*) _____ just over two years ago, notable improvements in productivity and quality (6 *notice*) _____. However, management is keen to take some of the criticism on board and has announced that the pay system (7 *review*) _____ in two months. Therefore, employees (8 *currently/encourage*) _____ to provide feedback on the system through informal channels of communication. Furthermore, a suggestions box (9 *also/provide*) _____ for anyone who wishes to make a proposal anonymously. The suggestions box (10 *can/find*) _____ next to the clocking-in machine by the staff notice board.

92

Self-study 5b

1 Put the following steps of the executive search process into the correct order.

- ❑ The client appoints one of the candidates.
- ❑ The headhunter identifies possible candidates.
- ❑ The candidates are interviewed by the headhunter.
- ❑ The client instructs the headhunter to fill a vacancy.
- ❑ The headhunter provides a shortlist of candidates.
- ❑ The client pays the headhunter his completion fee.
- ❑ Candidates go through the client's selection process.

2 Match the words as they appear in the unit.

1	recruitment	location
2	extension	agency
3	future	player
4	executive	shortage
5	neutral	reference
6	key	information
7	sensitive	search
8	skills	number

3 Complete each sentence with a suitable preposition.

1 Headhunting is _____ the increase as advertising becomes less and less cost-effective.

2 Headhunters are able to target people who are not actually _____ the job market.

3 A headhunter will always make a careful note of names _____ future reference.

4 Recruitment in the UK is divided _____ agency recruitment, advertising or executive search.

5 Headhunters can offer companies access _____ commercially sensitive information.

6 Executive search firms monitor internet forums, noting any interesting names they come _____ .

7 The headhunter assists _____ the offer process.

8 You don't need to be fed up _____ your job to be susceptible to an approach from a headhunter.

9 A brilliant contribution _____ an internet forum could possibly attract the attention of a headhunter.

4 Match the words.

1	fill	a list
2	present	a vacancy
3	shortlist	business
4	pay	findings
5	conduct	a retainer
6	compile	candidates

5 Use the words to write sentences with *recruit(ment)*.

Candidates go through our recruitment process.

apply   agency

qualities   candidates   process

sector   method

job   (**recruit(ment)**)   skills

CV   performance   shortlist

appoint   vacancy

headhunter

6 Complete the table.

Verb	Noun
apply	....
....	appointment
compare	....
explain	....
....	category
recruit	....

Reference words

7 Complete the text by filling each gap with a suitable reference word.

There are several methods a company can use when looking to fill staff vacancies. Each of (1) _these_ methods has its own advantages and disadvantages. When deciding (2) _____ of these to use, the company must first consider (3) _____ objectives. For instance, 'advertising selection', (4) _____ is placing an advertisement in a newspaper or magazine, is most suitable for (5) _____ vacancies which do not require particularly high levels of specialised knowledge. At the other end of the scale is the expensive process of 'executive search', (6) _____ is also known as 'headhunting'. (7) _____ method involves the company contracting a specialist to identify candidates (8) _____ best match its needs. Companies can only justify going to (9) _____ expense when they feel it will be difficult to fill a position using traditional methods. Between (10) _____ two extremes is a further method: agency recruitment.

Reading Test Part One

- Look at the sentences below and the five news bulletins.
- Which bulletin does each sentence refer to?
- For each sentence **1–8**, mark **one** letter **A**, **B**, **C**, **D** or **E**.
- You will need to use some of the letters more than once.

> **Example**
>
> **0** This company has suspended plans to work closely with another company.
>
>

1 This company will be working with a government organisation.
2 This company's decision to restructure will result in staff shortages.
3 This company is to reduce the number of administrative posts.
4 This company will sell off assets to offset poor financial results.
5 This company has made cuts which are unpopular with senior staff.
6 This company is in the process of upgrading some of its facilities.
7 This company has postponed its entry into new western European markets.
8 This company is suffering from the effects of increased competition.

A

> ### Taler to cut UK workforce
>
> Taler Chemicals, the Anglo-German industrial chemical company, announced yesterday that it is to cut 600 blue-collar jobs in a series of downsizing measures at three of its British plants. The news coincided with confirmation that the company also plans to dispose of its loss-making operations, CapPaints, the industrial solvent and paint division. This restructuring comes as the company reported a sharp drop in pre-tax profits. According to a company spokesman, the proposed joint venture with DTR International, one of Taler Chemicals' main competitors, is likely to be shelved.

B

> ### Merger creates Hungarian software powerhouse
>
> Silcom has finalised merger terms with ARER to create one of Hungary's largest computer software companies. Details of the merger are expected to be released later today. However, it is believed that Silcom's plans to break into France and Germany have been put on hold for the time being and that major job losses will soon be announced. Silcom looks set to benefit from the merger with ARER, which has recently been awarded a number of major contracts, including a contract with the Hungarian Ministry for Foreign Affairs, which will be worth in excess of $345,000 for the company.

C

> ### Profit warning at LYT International
>
> LYT International, one of Europe's leading Management Training Organisations, has warned shareholders to expect a fall in full year profits. The company, whose flagship training centre in Copenhagen is currently being modernised and refurbished, made an interim profit of $12m, compared with $23m in 2009. In response to its poor financial results, LYT has announced plans to cut jobs in its French and Spanish centres. An employee spokesman said that the move would prove unpopular and that with insufficient employees, some centres would struggle to deliver the high level of service demanded.

D

Shake-up at BTED

Nina Rantanen, former government adviser and the new CEO at BTED Power in Finland, has announced cost-cutting measures at the company. This decision has already led to the resignation of one of the company's most respected employees. Annika Ehlers had been with BTED Power for over twenty years, most recently as its Head of Operations. It is believed that she objected to company plans to reduce staffing levels at two of BTED Power's plants. Indications are that further high level resignations will follow in the next few months.

E

Restructuring plans announced at San Freight

San Freight has responded to redundancy rumours by revealing that it is to cut the number of office-based staff employed in its Scandinavian division by 25 per cent over the next twenty-four months. The announcement follows confirmation that the company has also decided to postpone the planned upgrading of haulage systems at its Stockholm subsidiary. A senior staff member has revealed that San Freight's business has deteriorated in recent months due to the escalating price war with central and eastern European rivals.

Reading Test Part Five

- Read the article below about corporate hospitality.
- For each question **1–10**, write **one** word.

Example

0

Corporate hospitality

In recent years there has been a noticeable growth in the number of operators offering corporate hospitality services. One of the most successful is *Truffles!*, which organises tailor-made corporate events (**0**) ..... varied as conferences and trade-fairs.

What makes *Truffles!* special is the way in (**1**) ..... the company carefully researches clients' needs and offers tailor-made advice. *Truffles!* also offers a wide range of supplementary services to complement its main venue-finding service, (**2**) ..... the majority of its competitors, who concentrate on the venue-finding side of the business.

Truffles! promises to find companies exactly the right setting for their corporate event, (**3**) ..... unusual the request may be. Venues include not (**4**) ..... the familiar large city centre hotels but also more unusual locations, such as wine cellars. *Truffles!* claims that (**5**) ..... of the venues it represents is checked regularly, which means that guests can be assured of consistently high standards.

Some of the most popular choices are the residential centres situated in the heart of Britain's finest countryside. One rarely finds, for example, as superb (**6**) ..... venue as *Watercress House* at such competitive rates. This elegant country house can accommodate up to 45 delegates in en suite rooms which include (**7**) ..... special features as direct-dial telephones, well-lit desks and modem sockets.

The main conference suite is located on the second floor and enjoys outstanding views over the surrounding countryside. Two further conference rooms are available, (**8**) ..... of which can accommodate up to twenty delegates.

Watercress House is just (**9**) ..... of the many splendid country houses represented by *Truffles!*, who currently have no fewer (**10**) ..... fifty such exceptional venues on their books.

Corporate culture

What shapes corporate culture?

Speaking

1 What can the following tell you about a company's culture?

- mission statement
- organisational hierarchy
- company buildings
- dress code

Reading

2 IKEA, the Swedish furniture retailer, promotes a single corporate culture throughout its international operations. Read the extract opposite from an IKEA brochure and make notes under the following headings.

Company values	
Company policies	
Staff profile	

A strong and living corporate culture

IKEA

IKEA has a strong and living corporate culture. It has grown step by step, bit by bit, along with our business idea. Our culture and business idea are the cornerstones of our operations. They support and strengthen each other. Our corporate culture helps us to retain the spirit and vitality of the early years, and to create a feeling of belonging in a large international organisation. Our corporate culture is what binds us together.

Our corporate culture is based on shared values: a simple and optimistic lifestyle, a natural way of working and being together, without imposing exaggerated respect and complicated regulations. The key words are simplicity and humility, thrift, a sense of responsibility, enthusiasm and flexibility. Perhaps the most important of these is simplicity, as seen in the unpretentious way we associate with each other. There are no status symbols to create barriers between managers and their fellow workers. Our customers don't expect to pay for first-class hotels, directors' dining rooms and flashy cars.

It is important that all employees share our basic values. We take a lot of trouble with recruitment. IKEA is an ideas company. Our business idea and culture provide us with a framework, and we look for people to build upon and promote our culture. But we also want people who can cut across our organisation, who are strong enough to question, renew and change. Such people promote development and should be encouraged not punished.

Internal promotion is still the norm, but we also recruit a number of people from outside. This is essential for strong expansion. And it provides us with new impulses.

Keeping our culture alive is management's key task. The best way is to set a good example and care about the employees. To see the person behind the professional. Caring means listening and encouraging new ideas and fresh initiatives, action and a sense of responsibility. Caring also means following up, putting right what goes wrong. Being able to praise and rebuke.

Our managers must know their job, and personally involve themselves in detail. 'Retail is detail.' Battles are seldom won at the desk. They are won out in the real world.

Simplicity and efficiency are usually synonymous concepts. Today we are a long way from our goals. We must put this right. At all levels. Then we will feel happier with each other and with our tasks. The continued success of IKEA rests on the involvement and enthusiasm of individual employees. And a great deal depends on our managers' perceptiveness and ability to care.

Language

3 Look at the gerund and infinitive in the following sentences. Find further examples of these forms in the text and discuss how they are used.

***Keeping** our culture alive is management's key task.*
*Our corporate culture helps us **to retain** the spirit and vitality of the early years.*

4 **In what ways is your own company culture similar or different to IKEA's?**

The IKEA way

1 **The Managing Director of IKEA UK talks about the company's corporate culture. Listen and choose one letter for the correct answer.**

1 How alike are all IKEA's stores worldwide?
  A Each store has the same management practices.
  B Each store carries a different product range.
  C Each store is adapted to the local culture.

2 What was the main influence on the formation of IKEA's values?
  A traditional Swedish values
  B Ingvar Kamprad's personal values
  C different cultural values within IKEA

3 IKEA can cope with the diversity of its workforce because
  A its managers have international experience.
  B its basic corporate values are found in all cultures.
  C its employees interpret IKEA's beliefs differently.

4 What is the main advantage of a strong corporate culture?
  A It makes international transfers easier.
  B It reduces the cost of global marketing.
  C It stops competitors copying IKEA.

5 What is IKEA's main policy for educating its staff?
  A It produces educational videos and brochures.
  B It holds special training sessions for managers.
  C It encourages regular meetings to discuss culture.

6 How does IKEA's culture affect its recruitment process?
  A Candidates are assessed on their personal qualities.
  B Highly skilled candidates are attracted to vacancies.
  C Candidates from a retail background are preferred.

7 What role does culture play in promotion decisions at IKEA?
   A Only Swedes can become senior managers.
   B A knowledge of Swedish culture is vital for promotion.
   C Nationality plays no part in promotion decisions.

8 Since the mid-1980s, IKEA's development has been most affected by the
   A stepping down of Ingvar Kamprad as President.
   B challenge of increasingly competitive markets.
   C way it has expanded over the last ten years.

Speaking **2** What does your company do to promote its corporate culture?

Listening 2 **3** Five IKEA managers talk about IKEA and its founder, Ingvar Kamprad. Listen and decide
1.26–1.30 which core IKEA values each anecdote illustrates.

   Speaker 1 .....

   Speaker 2 .....

   Speaker 3 .....

   Speaker 4 .....

   Speaker 5 .....

Speaking **4** Think of an anecdote to illustrate one of your company's core values.

Writing **5** Write a 200–250 word statement of your company's culture for the English version of a
      promotional brochure. Include information on your company's values and practices.

Optional task **6** Visit the www.ikea.com website and prepare a short presentation about IKEA's history and
      global expansion.

Cultural diversity

How culture influences business

Speaking

1 What factors affect decision-making in these areas in your country?

- recruiting new employees
- promoting staff
- fixing salary levels
- making staff redundant

Reading 1

2 Look at the article on the opposite page about a research project which examines the effect of cultural values on management decision-making. Choose the best sentence to fill each gap.

A This relationship is based on shared expectations which are common to employees of the same nationality.

B Typical of this is the belief that individuals should receive salary gains without having to share them with lower-performance colleagues.

C These take the form of one-page problem scenarios, each one centred on a specific issue.

D However, without this awareness, employees from diverse nationalities cannot appreciate their differences and build mutual understanding.

E Most international human resources managers will have experienced these expectation differences at first hand.

F These sensitive areas touch directly upon cultural norms and people's sense of well-being and order.

G Decisions taken with the welfare of more than the individual in mind are characteristic of this value system.

H There is also the more complicated question: what reasons do they give to explain their choices?

Speaking

3 Are decisions affecting each of the four areas based on group or market logic in your culture?

National cultures, international business

National culture is a major barrier to making global businesses effective. Different nationalities have different expectations as to how employers and employees should behave. Michaël Segalla describes how national values are directly related to organisational decision-making.

In today's hyper-competitive global markets, any company that operates internationally is faced with the task of integrating many value systems into a
5 framework that allows the organisation not only to survive but also to compete effectively. A European research group – the European Managerial Decision Making Project – was
10 formed in 1994 to examine the effect of different national value systems on organisational policy. The project's research methodology is simple: given identical business problems, do
15 managers in six different European countries choose similar solutions? 0 H In addition to the responses to these two questions, the study also includes both organisational and
20 personal data.

The behaviours that intrigue the research team most are decisions concerning recruitment, promotion, remuneration and workforce
25 reductions. The criteria used to select, promote, pay and make employees redundant are thought to reveal most about national values. 1 Decisions about finance and
30 marketing, on the other hand, are far less emotive and less likely to reveal underlying values.

The researchers believe a strong bond exists between people's sense
35 of well-being and their situation at work, that is, the way they get on with a work group or employer. 2 For multinationals, therefore, an understanding of cultural
40 diversity within the organisation is a prerequisite of effective employee relationships.

The research is based on semi-structured interviews with managers
45 from seventy-four European banks. The managers are presented with common dilemmas focusing on the four key areas: recruitment, promotion, remuneration and reductions in the
50 workforce. 3 The respondents are asked to solve these dilemmas and give their reasoning.

The responses are then plotted between two opposing logics. The
55 first is called 'group logic'. 4 Even decisions such as who to promote or make redundant can sometimes be discussed in terms of their group effects. The second logic
60 is an economic rationale, which the researchers called 'market logic'. Here decisions are based on the economic realities arising from the marketplace as opposed to group
65 considerations. 5 A summary of the study's findings is shown in Figure 1 (on the next page).

According to research, few people really know their own cultural values.
70 6 This means that organisations need to approach cross-cultural training seriously as it can be critical to the success of an international venture. Simply bringing in a 'cultural
75 expert' to talk about different national values is not an option. Although these seminars can be entertaining, they ultimately fail because they do not require managers to examine their own
80 values first.

Adapted from the *Financial Times*

4 Read the conclusions below from the European Managerial Decision Making Project. Which country does each colour refer to?

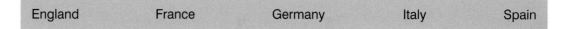

| England | France | Germany | Italy | Spain |

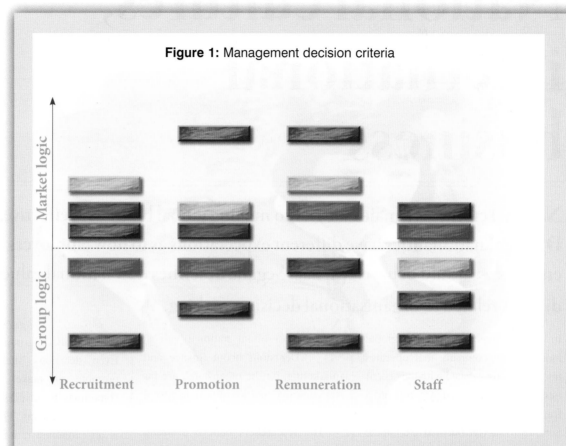

Figure 1: Management decision criteria

The results of the survey are summarised below.

• In Italy, England and France respondents tended to use market logic in hiring new managers. They more often chose to hire foreign, multilingual employees with an elite general education. The German and Spanish managers followed the opposite strategy by hiring local managers with more technical training.

• The German sample stood nearly alone in its concern for promoting managers on the basis of objective performance criteria. In contrast, French managers based promotion on seniority or group loyalty criteria.

• The German sample stood alone again in its concern that remuneration should be based on measurable individual performance factors. Again the French sample held the extreme opposite belief that remuneration should be based on group, not individual performance.

• English managers most often based staff reduction decisions on the performance-to-salary ratio. More than 70 per cent of the English respondents would make redundant a middle-aged, high-salary manager with average performance. At the opposite end of the scale, less than 10 per cent of the German respondents would discharge the same manager. They would favour discharging young managers who could find jobs more easily, thereby preserving social stability.

Speaking

5 Choose two of the five countries. What difficulties might people from these countries experience when working together?

Building international teams

Speaking

1 Work in groups. Your company is entering into an overseas joint venture. First decide on the details of the companies involved (nationalities, activities etc.). Then read the following email and decide on a recruitment policy.

International Sales

From: Jocelyn Garvie, Human Resources
Sent: 22 January 2011 09:59
To:
Subject: Recruitment policy for new joint venture

We need to discuss the management team for the new joint venture. We've decided we need a team of four but haven't thought about personal profiles yet. I've organised a meeting for next Tuesday and I suggest we think about the following issues.

- Ideal age, sex and nationality of the team members
- Recruitment policy (internal, national or international)
- Hierarchy and communication within the team
- Pay structure for the team members

Could you think about it and have some proposals ready for Tuesday? We'll be starting at 10 am. The meeting will be conducted in English as usual.

 **Don't forget**

Agreeing and disagreeing

We often show agreement by repeating other people's words or completing their sentences. We can reinforce a proposal by adding supporting ideas.

- *I think that's the best way of doing it.*
- ▼ *I think that's the best way too. And it would save money.*
- *I think we should pay team bonuses.*
- ▼ *Which would encourage team spirit as well.*

In order to disagree effectively, it is important to give reasons or ask questions.

- *It would be a good idea to recruit internationally.*
- ▼ *That's true. But it would be more expensive.*
- *I think it's important to use Head Office staff.*
- ▼ *But who would you choose?*

Writing

2 Write a 200–250 word letter to a business partner visiting your country. Give advice about attitudes to hierarchy, time, gender and anything else you think is important.

Optional task

3 Choose a country and research the cultural attitudes which might affect the way you would do business there. Prepare a brief presentation on your findings.

Self-study 6a

1 Choose the correct word to fill each gap.

The number of training organisations in the country has been increasing at a rapid (1) _____ over the last decade and this trend seems set to continue. Management Worldwide Ltd is one of the country's most (2) _____ training organisations, with over 50 centres throughout the UK. Its focus is on a (3) _____ area: management skills training. Management Worldwide employs over a thousand people in areas as (4) _____ as accountancy, marketing, computing, sales and languages. It has a non-hierarchical approach to management and believes in giving (5) _____ to staff at all levels of the organisation. Its corporate (6) _____, as stated in the company's mission (7) _____ , include optimism, respect and flexibility. Management Worldwide's business goal is to increase shareholder value by concentrating on its (8) _____ training business and offering excellent service to clients.

1	A pace	B speed	C initiative
2	A successful	B exaggerated	C valuable
3	A reduced	B single	C uniform
4	A irregular	B flexible	C diverse
5	A initiative	B pressure	C responsibility
6	A strategies	B values	C qualities
7	A statement	B catalogue	C brochure
8	A core	B essential	C prime

2 Complete each sentence with the correct form of the word in capital letters.

1 ADAPT
We've only made minor product _____ for the North American market.

2 COMPETE
In the past, several of IKEA's _____ have tried to clone the company's store concept.

3 OPERATE
The company actively promotes a single company culture throughout its international _____ .

4 PROMOTE
The marketing division has produced a very flashy _____ brochure for the campaign.

5 INTERPRET
Some cultures may have different _____ of concepts like freedom and authority.

6 EXPAND
The rapid pace of _____ has had a big influence on the way the company has developed.

7 INFLUENCE
Our new CEO has been very _____ in reshaping our corporate culture.

8 PERCEIVE
I find her really _____ ; she notices what's going on, even when it's not obvious.

3 Match the words with a similar meaning.

1	diverse	new
2	similar	different
3	informal	hard
4	fresh	crucial
5	economical	worldwide
6	vital	thrifty
7	tough	casual
8	global	alike

Gerunds and infinitives

4 Complete the text. Put each verb in brackets into the correct form.

Birte Soltvedt has been the Managing Director of Denpak for five years now and it is easy (1 see) to see the influence she has had in that time. Upon (2 arrive) _____ at Denpak, Soltvedt went about fundamentally modernising the Danish packaging company's way of (3 operate) _____ as well as (4 restructure) _____ its management. Although this came as a shock to many managers used to (5 work) _____ within a very strict hierarchy, the new, flatter management structure has helped Denpak (6 increase) _____ efficiency while (7 realise) _____ substantial cost savings at the same time. Considered by many (8 be) _____ a hard and uncompromising businesswoman, the 46-year-old Norwegian is happy enough (9 let) _____ people (10 believe) _____ this, even though she herself insists that in reality she really dislikes (11 confront) _____ people and worries about every decision she makes. Despite successfully managing (12 turn) _____ the company around, Soltvedt says there is no time (13 reflect) _____ on her achievements. Instead, she is busily planning the company's long-term growth strategy and implementing even more changes: 'It's essential that we keep (14 look) _____ to the future. The worst thing Denpak could possibly do now is stop (15 modernise) _____ just because the company happens (16 be) _____ back in profit.'

Self-study 6b

1 Complete the text with the following linking words and phrases.

while	therefore	however	similarly
means that	as opposed to		although

Increased exposure to international business (**1**) _____ Japanese companies are not always as traditional as in the past. (**2**) _____ , there are still a number of important cultural factors which need to be considered when doing business in Japan.

- During negotiations, it is common for there to be long periods of silence (**3**) _____ your Japanese colleagues formulate their response.

- The Japanese will still usually avoid saying 'no'. You may (**4**) _____ leave a meeting with the wrong impression.

- Japanese meetings tend to be more formal than those in the USA, with people being addressed by their title and surname (**5**) _____ their first names.

- Dress is a very important issue for the Japanese, with a smart suit and tie the expected dress code in all business situations.

- Business remains still very much a male domain and (**6**) _____ inroads have been made by Japanese women, it is still unusual to find them in high level positions. (**7**) _____ , workers in senior positions tend to be older than their counterparts in the USA.

2 The graph shows the changing number of employees at two multinationals, 2006–2010. Write a 120–140 word report describing and comparing the two companies.

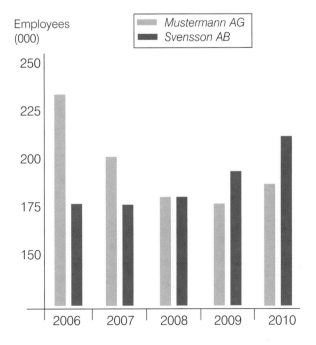

3 Match the words as they appear in the unit.

1	do	differences
2	fix	business
3	conduct	a strategy
4	appreciate	a belief
5	build	salary levels
6	solve	understanding
7	follow	a meeting
8	hold	a dilemma

4 Complete the table.

Verb	Noun
choose	....
....	success
expect	....
....	effect
pay	....
believe	....
....	solution
promote	....
....	diversity
examine	....
....	preservation

Modals

5 Use the exact form of the verb in brackets to rewrite the following sentences.

1 Perhaps the name of the product was the problem.
(*could*) The name of the product could have been the problem.

2 It was a waste of time going there.
(*needn't*)
_____

3 Adapting the product was a bad decision.
(*should*)
_____

4 It's time we were getting back.
(*ought*)
_____

5 Well, the language problems didn't help, did they?
(*can't*)
_____

6 Maybe they're having trouble working together.
(*might*)
_____

Reading Test Part Three

- Read the following article on business ethics and the questions on the opposite page.
- Each question has four suggested answers or ways of finishing the sentence, **A**, **B**, **C** and **D**.
- Mark **one** letter **A**, **B**, **C** or **D** for the answer you choose.

Companies turn to ethics for competitive advantage

In the old days measuring company performance was simply a case of looking at turnover, profits and dividends. However, the last few years have seen environmental and ethical issues move to the forefront of public concern and resulted in a closer scrutiny of a company's performance in terms of its business ethics. As the Government has been slow to respond to the increasing importance of ethics, companies have been forced to address the subject themselves and re-align their own management policies accordingly. These policies will determine how a company conducts all aspects of its business, from dealing with clients to reporting to shareholders.

By setting themselves up as ethical, however, companies are not so much promoting the importance of ethical conduct, the well-being of the local community or the development of society as a whole, as engaging in a powerful marketing and PR exercise to attract both discerning clients and bright young recruits. In today's markets, any company without a coherent ethics policy is in danger of surrendering a competitive advantage to its rivals.

In order to develop an ethical code of conduct, companies will have to deal with issues such as the legal implications of their disciplinary measures and the effect any new procedures will have on employees. However, new policies can only be developed once the company has identified the core values that underpin its day to day operations. Without a clear understanding of these values, it is impossible to develop a code of conduct compatible with the company's culture. An effective code will dictate how employees approach conflicts and other stressful dilemmas not covered by the normal terms and conditions of employment. It will provide employees with a clear understanding of what behaviour is expected when they find themselves confronted with such dilemmas.

Ethical procedures are particularly critical in times of crisis. Pay disputes, sexual harassment charges or cases of fraud, for example, can involve very complex issues that require careful decision-making and can have a very negative effect on staff morale. At such times it is crucial that companies act in an ethical manner. By doing so, they may not be able to avoid the potentially damaging publicity such cases inevitably attract; they will, however, be in a much stronger position to defend themselves in a court of law.

The major obstacle which companies face, having established a code of conduct, is that of ensuring that each individual member of staff follows it. Some organisations simply distribute leaflets to all staff in the hope that they will read and act on them. Other companies take a more active approach and invite management gurus to hold seminars on the subject, which, while often highly entertaining, have little long-term impact. Although some companies now include ethics as part of their standard induction programme, it is widely accepted that this is not enough. The issue of ethics in the workplace is now of such importance that it needs to be incorporated into in-company development programmes for all employees, from the shop floor to the boardroom.

With little sign of public concern abating, no organisation can afford to ignore the subject of ethics in the workplace. In order to address the issue effectively, companies need to ensure that staff at all levels feel committed to the company and its values and are motivated to transfer this commitment into ethical behaviour.

1   Business ethics are becoming more important as a result of

    A consumer demands.

    B shareholder concern.

    C management theories.

    D government legislation.

2   Why are companies promoting ethical practice?

    A to develop customer awareness of social issues

    B to help raise money for the local community

    C to enhance the positive image of the company

    D to improve the conduct of employees

3   What must companies do first to develop an ethical code?

    A take appropriate legal advice

    B consult employees at all levels

    C establish their basic principles

    D set up disciplinary procedures

4   A code of conduct helps employees

    A work together more effectively.

    B improve terms and conditions.

    C understand their duties better.

    D cope with difficult situations.

5   At times of crisis, a code of conduct reduces the

    A likelihood of negative publicity.

    B potential damage of legal action.

    C negative effect on staff morale.

    D time it takes to make decisions.

6   How can companies ensure that staff follow ethical procedures?

    A by distributing detailed leaflets to employees

    B by integrating ethics into training at all levels

    C by arranging seminars with ethics consultants

    D by including ethics in induction programmes

Writing Test Part Two (A)

- Your company is experiencing financial difficulties. Your manager has asked you to write a report considering ways of cutting costs in your department.
- Write a **report**, suggesting ways of cutting costs and explaining the implications these cuts might have on the running of your department.
- Write **200–250** words.

Reading Test Part Four

- Read the article below about cultural awareness in business.
- Choose the best word to fill each gap.
- For each question **1–10**, mark **one** letter **A**, **B**, **C** or **D**.
- There is an example at the beginning (**0**).

Cultural awareness

To succeed in today's global market place, it is essential to learn as much as possible about the (**0**) ..... in overseas markets. In the past, companies with international aspirations simply familiarised themselves with any differences in the legal system or in the (**1**) ..... used in the day-to-day business of import and export.

Modern trade, however, (**2**) ..... more. Today the company seeking international success must also understand the people who live and work in countries they deal with, how they think, behave and do business. In short, today's market leaders must (**3**) ..... greater cultural awareness.

Business people operating in foreign markets often fail to consider that cultural differences can result in a (**4**) ..... of approaches to everyday business activities such as the way a cross-cultural team (**5**) ..... or how it conducts its meetings.

One of the main (**6**) ..... of investing in our cultural awareness programmes is that they can help you to fully (**7**) ..... your business potential, leaving you better placed to succeed. Our cultural awareness training seminars will (**8**) ..... the importance of taking into account how other nationalities think and behave and how they might see you. We can also help you develop the (**9**) ..... you need to construct effective working relationships and (**10**) ..... difficulties that may arise when working with colleagues or clients from different nationalities and cultures.

Example

0   **A** conditions   **B** elements   **C** influences   **D** factors

A   B   C   D
■   ☐   ☐   ☐

	A	**B**	**C**	**D**
1	technicalities	mechanics	schedules	procedures
2	commands	requests	demands	prescribes
3	procure	find	acquire	earn
4	variety	scope	choice	selection
5	co-operates	associates	contributes	participates
6	prizes	benefits	premiums	compensations
7	practice	exploit	outdo	employ
8	demonstrate	expose	announce	publish
9	talent	skills	strength	proficiencies
10	overturn	overrun	overtake	overcome

Exam practice

Reading Test Part Five

- Read the article below about effective negotiating.
- For each question **1–10**, write **one** word.

Example

0 A L S O

Effective negotiating

We are always negotiating, not only in business, but **(0)** ..... in our private lives, from deciding what to watch on TV to deciding where to go on holiday. Rarely, in fact, **(1)** ..... any form of decision reached without some form of negotiation.

But **(2)** ..... we practise the art on a regular basis, it is always useful to review what we already subconsciously know. The following tips provide you **(3)** ..... strategies for negotiating effectively, no matter **(4)** ..... situation you find yourself in.

Firstly, try to make it a win-win situation. Start with the attitude that all parties should get something out of the deal. Look at the common ground, **(5)** ..... only at the gaps between you.

Secondly, try to find out what is cheap for you but valuable to your negotiating partner and vice versa. Exchanging something you don't want **(6)** ..... something you actually do want is, of course, the aim of **(7)** ..... parties involved.

Thirdly, be aware of your BATNA, your 'Best Alternative to a Negotiated Agreement'. You won't always get **(8)** ..... very deal you wanted so you need to bear in mind your best alternative if the negotiation fails. In fact, telling your negotiating partner, 'Thanks but I can get a better deal elsewhere' often brings about movement in the other side's position!

And finally, be creative. Think of the exercise **(9)** ..... both sides coming together to solve a common problem. Developing the valuable skills you need to negotiate most effectively takes time and effort, but by taking on just a **(10)** ..... simple techniques, you can make all the difference.

Writing Test Part Two (B)

- A trainee from one of your company's overseas subsidiaries is coming to work as your assistant for six months. Your boss has asked you to brief her on your company before she arrives.
- Write a **letter** to the trainee, describing the organisation of your company, the people she needs to know and the kind of work she will be doing. Include any further useful information which you think the trainee should know about your company.
- Write **200–250** words.

Industrial espionage

Research or espionage?

Speaking

1 How can a company access information about competitors? Which methods do you think are ethically acceptable?

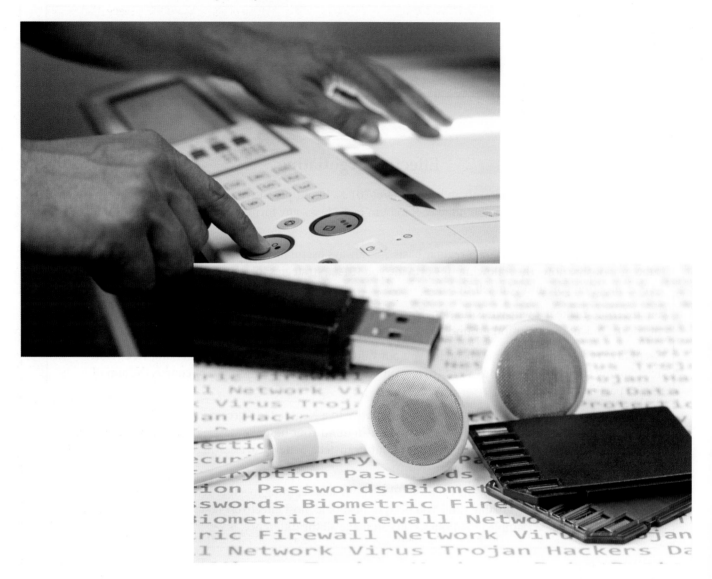

Reading

2 Read the jumbled newspaper article on the opposite page. What methods are mentioned in the article?

3 Now put the paragraphs into the correct order.

1	C.	6	....
2	....	7	....
3	....	8	....
4	....	9	....
5	....	10	....

Documents, Data and Discovery

A   The court case involving Mr Lee has revealed to us the secretive world of industrial espionage – that is the dishonest or illicit ways in which a company, or someone acting for them can interfere with their competitors operations, or discover what they wish to keep secret.

B   Other examples can be even stranger. One European engineering company was hosting a visitor from a company in Asia. It was noticed that he frequently stopped to tie up his shoelaces, even when it didn't appear necessary. What he was actually doing was collecting minute pieces of waste metal from the factory floor on a piece of tape attached to his lace. The intention was to take the metal back to his company for analysis in their laboratory.

C   Lee Yung-fa was leaving the USA, returning home to Taipei, when he was taken out of the queue by Customs Officers for a random search. To the surprise of the custom officers, they found thousands of electronic documents, all of a confidential nature in his baggage. He had copied them onto discs and was taking them back to Taipei. The 35-year old IT specialist had been working for an American electronics company for three years, and had left the company the previous week, after completing his contract.

D   Companies do try to find out what their competitors are planning, and most of this intelligence gathering is perfectly legitimate. It is common practice for companies to collect scraps of information at conferences and trade shows. However, talk to any major player in any industry and they will tell you illicit intelligence gathering is increasing and will continue to do so.

E   Having said that, attempts to prevent rivals discovering confidential information, or even the theft of technology is always likely to be a major part of a company's plans to remain competitive. This is especially true in the technology rich fields of engineering, where the leading companies, from the developed world, already have a technological advantage.

F   Industrial spies are increasingly using electronic methods of gaining access to information. This may involve secretly recording conversations – bugging – or hacking into secure databases. Companies and government agencies alike are concerned with the threat of cyber-espionage. Although, officials in many countries are unwilling to comment officially about how they are dealing with the threat.

G   He is being accused, by his former employers in the US, of being 'secretly involved' in the development of new products for a company in his homeland while he was under contract to his American employers. The Taiwanese company in question has refused to comment on the case.

H   There are a number of ways that companies use to discover their rival's secrets. One of the most common ways of getting hold of secrets is for employees to take them to a rival, when they change jobs. This can be done by something as simple as photocopying internal documents. Anders Johannsen, CEO of Svalk, a Swedish high-tech engineering firm has seen it all before. "Three or four times in the last three years, we have seen our technical secrets in use in a rival's product. The only explanation is that when one of our employees has moved to another company in the same industry, they have taken details of our designs along with them." There seems to be little Svalk and companies like it can do, legally, given that finding evidence to prove the theft is extremely difficult.

I   How can companies protect themselves from industrial espionage? Every company wants to prevent leaks of inside information and one solution is to establish a complex set of safeguards to prevent leaks from IT sources, or even the old fashioned approach of keeping things under lock and key. An alternative solution is to simply assume that information will leak out and to focus attention on making the company's products so complicated, or so loaded with security devices that they are impossible to copy. Peter Wolfarth, spokesman for consortium of British Software companies working in Asia does not worry about software theft. "We have better things to do than worry about intellectual property", he says, "when we are trying to be more innovative more quickly than our rivals."

J   Espionage between companies has shot up to the position of supreme importance to most, if not all of the world's leading companies as the rate of technological change increases. As change become more and more rapid, companies are increasingly anxious to gain access to their rival's new secrets as early as they can in the race to be the first to market with new products and services.

Adapted from the *Financial Times*

4 Look at some of these common reasons for industrial espionage. Can you think of any more? Which do you think are the most likely reasons for espionage in your company?

| money | ideology | ego | personal relationships with someone in a rival company |

5 What could your company do to reduce the risk of industrial espionage?

Information security

1 Rick Haywood, Managing Director of electronics wholesaler Octacon, discusses
1.31 information security with two colleagues. Listen and identify the problem.

2 Listen to the rest of the discussion and complete the table.
1.32

Action discussed	Implications

Language

3 Look at the conditional forms in the following sentences. Find further examples of these forms in the audioscripts and discuss how they are used.

If there genuinely *is* a problem, then we*'ll have* to find out ...
If I *knew* that, we *wouldn't be* here.

4 Complete the following information with phrases from the audioscripts.

Don't forget

Asking for clarification

The following phrases are useful when asking for clarification.

Are you saying ... ?
_____
_____
_____
_____

Speaking

5 Your company wants to create a more open attitude towards internal information. Discuss and decide the following.

• what information should be available to staff
• the implications of the new policy

Your teacher will give you some cards with instructions.

Business ethics

What are business ethics?

Speaking

1 Which of the following statements about ethics do you agree with?

- Ethics provide the rules within which an organisation must conduct itself.
- Ethics show an organisation's attitude towards society.
- Ethics are a source of competitive advantage.

Reading

2 Read the extract on the opposite page from the Deerwode Ethical Practice report. What did the CEOs consider the three most important features of an ethical organisation?

3 Read the extract again. Are the following statements true or false?

1 The questionnaire was sent to a total of 500 senior executives.
2 It was thought to be of great importance to support good causes.
3 Fewer than half of the participating companies protect whistle-blowers.
4 Most CEOs were content with existing information security measures.

Language

4 Look at the report again and find examples of the following.

DEERWODE
Ethical practice in the workplace

Summary of findings

In April 2010, a questionnaire was sent to the CEOs and senior managers of 500 UK companies, which had been selected on the basis of size in terms of number of employees. In response to an increasing level of interest expressed by managers in the public sector led us to extend our sample to include the senior executives of a further 20 organisations in the public sector, most of whom were involved in working with the health sector in some way.

Key Findings

According to the survey, when executives described an organisation as 'highly ethical', the factors considered most important were fair employment practices, legal compliance and the delivery of high-quality goods and services. Corporate philanthropy was given the least weight in making this judgement.

It was found that 38% of the organisations surveyed had formal policies to protect employees who report ethical or legal violations, i.e. whistle blowers, an increase of 22% reported in the previous survey. In total, written statements of values and principles were produced by 85% of participating organizations.

Deerwode devised a list of issues relating to company integrity against which managers had to indicate the level of attention each issue received in their organisation. The results can be seen below. Of these issues, the two most frequently identified as of greatest concern for the next three to five years were security of information and environmental issues. Security of information was also the issue with which respondents were least satisfied with current efforts.

London, May 2011

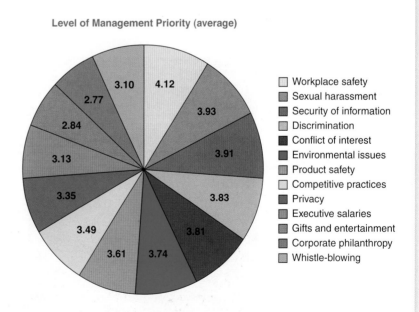

Level of Management Priority (average)

- Workplace safety
- Sexual harassment
- Security of information
- Discrimination
- Conflict of interest
- Environmental issues
- Product safety
- Competitive practices
- Privacy
- Executive salaries
- Gifts and entertainment
- Corporate philanthropy
- Whistle-blowing

Speaking   **5 Which ethical issues are you most concerned about in your company?**

Ethical issues

1 Five people talk about unethical behaviour at their companies. Listen and decide which ethical issue and which consequence each speaker refers to.

Task one: ethical issue
Which ethical issue does each speaker refer to?

1 .....

2 .....

3 .....

4 .....

5 .....

A industrial espionage
B workplace safety
C racial discrimination
D environmental protection
E executive salaries
F sexual harassment
G financial mismanagement
H corporate gift-giving

Task two: consequence
Which consequence does each speaker refer to?

6 .....

7 .....

8 .....

9 .....

10 .....

I a manager was dismissed
J computer security was reviewed
K an ethics officer was appointed
L the company informed the police
M a written warning was given
N the company produced guidelines
O a consultant was brought in
P the employee resigned

Speaking   **2** Now put the five cases of unethical behaviour into order of seriousness.

Language

3 Look at the conditional forms in the following sentences. Find further examples of these forms in the audioscript and discuss how they are used.

If she'd complained to him in person, he'd have stopped doing it.
She warned them that she'd take legal action if nothing was done about it.

Speaking 1.38–1.39

4 Talk about one of the following topics for one minute.

- how to encourage ethical behaviour from employees
- the importance of ethics in today's business world

MORE MONEY FLOWS INTO ETHICAL INVESTMENT FUNDS

Neil James is optimistic about the current trend of investment in the UK

Companies face increased pressure on ethical reporting

Sarah Arnold reports on the Department de and Industry's latest guidelines

JOB FITNESS TEST RULED AS DISCRIMINATION

crimination in the work place. Lucy Burgess

Banks accused of discrimination against ethnic minorities

In a major new survey on discrimination

HOME NEWS 10

Over 50s still face widespread discrimination

Michael Price watches with concern as t nort expo

5

More companies now accept the concept of business ethics

emary Westgate reports on the f ompani

Optional task

5 Use the internet to find out about a company that has been accused of ethical misconduct. Write a 200–250 word report on the case, suggesting what could have been done to prevent it and what measures could still be put in place.

Self-study 7a

1 Are the following examples of industrial espionage or measures against it?

1. infiltrate a competitor
2. monitor photocopier use
3. bug an office
4. hack into a network
5. shred important documents
6. leak sensitive information
7. bring in a security adviser
8. steal confidential data
9. identify a perpetrator
10. resort to shady practices
11. protect a computer system
12. install passwords

2 Some of the following lines contain an unnecessary word. Underline any extra words in lines 1–13.

1 Octacon, the electronics wholesaler, is worried about
2 this information security within the company. It has
3 recently lost several of major contracts to Centronics,
4 to its largest competitor. Centronics seems to have
5 been acquired information regarding the terms and
6 conditions of Octacon's existing contracts. It has
7 targeted customers each time their contracts were
8 up for renewal. Octacon suspects that a disgruntled
9 employee who has been leaking crucial details to
10 their competitor or that Centronics has managed to
11 infiltrate by Octacon, for example by hacking into their
12 corporate intranet. This would be illegal, of course, but
13 without a proof there is little Octacon can do.

3 Complete the table.

Verb	Noun	Adjective
....	....	acceptable
suspect	....	....
....	imitation	....
access	....	....
analyse	....	....
....	security	....
protect	....	....
....	copy	....
identify	....	....
confuse	....	....
isolate	....	....
....	....	broken
measure	....	....

4 Match the words as they appear in the unit.

1. solve — a problem
2. call — paperwork
3. bear — measures
4. devise — a grudge
5. break — foul play
6. suspect — the police
7. shred — the law
8. take — a system

Conditionals

5 Complete the conversation. Put each verb in brackets into the correct form.

● Jill, it's Rick. I'm just calling to see whether you've come across anything in those appraisal files.

▼ Well, there are one or two interesting things but nothing shocking. If you (**1** *have*) ____have____ a moment, I (**2** *come by*) __can come by__ and show you what I've found so far.

● Well, I'm just about to go into a meeting right now. But if you (**3** *be*) _____ free this afternoon, we (**4** *go*) _____ through it then. Why don't you give Oliver a call and see if he (**5** *be*) _____ around, as well?

▼ He's not in today. He's having a day off.

● That's a shame because it (**6** *be*) _____ good if we (**7** *also/look*) _____ at what he's found on the email server.

▼ I (**8** *give*) _____ him a call at home if you (**9** *like*) _____ . He might be in.

● Good idea. Maybe he's got some print-outs or something in his desk which you could bring along.

▼ OK. But if he (**10** *not/have*) _____ anything, (**11** *you/still want*) _____ us to meet this afternoon?

● Yes. I mean, if he (**12** *not/find*) _____ anything worth mentioning last week, then he (**13** *not/need*) _____ come along to the meeting anyway.

▼ That's true. What if he (**14** *have*) _____ got something, though?

● Well, is he back tomorrow?

▼ I think so, yes.

● OK, call him first. If he (**15** *find*) _____ something, then we (**16** *put*) _____ the meeting off until tomorrow.

▼ OK. I'll get back to you when I've spoken to him.

1 Read through the unit and add more ethical issues.

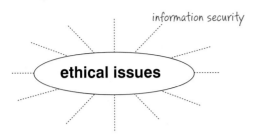

information security

ethical issues

Which issues do the following refer to?

1 employees copying confidential data onto disks
   information security

2 physically intimidating the opposite sex

3 accidents occurring at work

4 conforming to government legislation

5 senior managers receiving massive pay increases

6 rewarding clients with expensive freebies

7 not treating people from ethnic minorities equally

8 reporting breaches of a company's ethical code

2 Add a prefix to form the opposite of the following.

1 legal   ....
2 ethical   ....
3 fair   ....
4 lawful   ....
5 correct   ....
6 official   ....

3 Match the words with a similar meaning.

1 survey   precaution
2 measure   questionnaire
3 conduct   gift
4 rule   competitor
5 threat   regulation
6 rival   behaviour
7 freebie   warning

4 Fill each gap with a suitable word.

As you know, our company had been doing business out there for years, working with the smaller family-run firms. Nigel Beynon, (**1**) _____ was the Head of Purchasing for over fifteen years, had managed (**2**) _____ build up several solid relationships with local suppliers. In fact, I sometimes thought he felt (**3**) _____ at home out there than he (**4**) _____ back here in the UK. Anyway, problems first arose (**5**) _____ one of the newspapers decided to do a feature (**6**) _____ ethics in the clothing industry. They discovered (**7**) _____ one of our suppliers was using child labour. It was (**8**) _____ much of a shock to Nigel as it was to everyone (**9**) _____ . You see, he'd never actually visited (**10**) _____ single factory. He'd just believed the suppliers (**11**) _____ they assured him they conformed to our workplace standards. If only he (**12**) _____ taken the time to check their claims, he'd never have had to hand in his notice.

Conditionals

5 Complete the sentences. Put each verb in brackets into the correct form.

1 If she (*realise*) _'d realised_ the report was confidential, she (*not/tell*) _wouldn't have told_ her friend about it.

2 The boss (*sack*) _____ him by now if he (*not/be*) _____ the Managing Director's nephew.

3 If we (*not/get*) _____ that contract, the company (*not/survive*) _____ the recession last year.

4 I'm sure she (*dismiss*) _____ if anyone (*find out*) _____ how she was getting her information.

5 If she (*not/film*) _____ shredding the files, she (*still/work*) _____ here today.

6 The problem (*solve*) _____ more quickly if the company (*bring*) _____ in a consultant earlier.

7 The company (*not/know*) _____ if the new assistant (*not/blow*) _____ the whistle to the press.

8 If he (*leave*) _____ sooner than he did, the company (*not/have*) _____ all the bad publicity it is right now.

Reading Test Part Two

- Read the health and safety guidelines.
- Choose the best sentence from **A–H** to fill in each of the gaps.
- For each gap **1–6**, mark one letter **A–H**.
- Do not mark any letter more than once.
- There is an example at the beginning (**0**).

Health and Safety Guidelines – Visual Display Units (VDUs)

In order to eliminate risk to the health and safety of employees, appliances should be used in accordance with suppliers' and manufacturers' instructions. As far as is reasonably practicable, all appliances should be kept in a good state of repair. **0** H Any appliance which is consequently found to be faulty or potentially dangerous should, where possible, be immediately isolated from the electrical supply and reported to a supervisor.

It is required by law that employees using VDUs should have regular breaks. **1** In both cases supervisors are responsible for ensuring that these breaks are observed. The company provides word processors which have been specially selected to provide a safe system of work and every effort has been made to ensure that they have been ergonomically designed. **2** This may be due to individual physical characteristics of the operator rather than the machine itself. In such cases, the company is obliged to take every action to improve the situation.

All employees are expected to notify their manager about any discomfort experienced whilst using a word processor. **3** Where entries refer to eyesight, display screen users are entitled, upon request, to a free eye test, the cost to be met by the company. If a user is said by his/her optician to require frequent eye tests, the employer should meet the costs of all necessary tests. **4** Operators are otherwise entitled to one free eye test every twelve months unless there are exceptional medical circumstances which have arisen during the period between examinations.

The development of office networks has resulted in modular configurations, comprising a number of interchangeable computers which may be easily moved around. **5** Moreover, employees should take care to ensure that no undue strain is caused through lifting in the wrong way.

It is the responsibility of all employees to report accidents. **6** This may help prevent a more serious incident from happening in the future.

A Any such complaints should be recorded in the company's Health and Safety log book.

B A supervisor should be notified immediately of all occurrences, however minor, so that appropriate action can be taken.

C These should be taken regardless of whether they follow a period of intense or occasional use.

D Attention is drawn to the possible dangers in seeking to carry too heavy a load.

E However, in some cases, the operation of such equipment can have an adverse effect.

F Hazards such as these must be reported immediately to the manager or any other person authorised to act on his or her behalf.

G This provision is restricted to situations where the need arises because of the employee's work.

H For this reason, visual display equipment should be regularly checked for damage.

Reading Test Part Six

- In **most** lines of the following text, there is **one** unnecessary word. It is either grammatically incorrect or does not fit in with the sense of the text.
- For each numbered line **1–12**, find the unnecessary word. Some lines are correct. If a line is correct, write **CORRECT**.
- The exercise begins with two examples (**0**) and (**00**).

Example

0	C	O	R	R	E	C	T		
00	L	O	N	G					

Working overseas

0	We are currently recruiting engineers, nurses, teachers and managers for
00	placements of six months long in a variety of locations worldwide.
1	Working overseas can offer you a once in a lifetime opportunity to live,
2	work and build the friendships in a very different environment. This
3	experience which will also give you a chance to widen your outlook on life,
4	encounter with cultural differences and develop new skills. To join us, you
5	must be fully qualified and have at least two years' full-time experience. In
6	addition to being resourceful, and you must be able to show sensitivity to
7	cultural differences. Flexibility that is also an extremely important quality;
8	you should be able to imagine what yourself happily adapting to new
9	standards of behaviour and dress, different food and even opening hours.
10	We will provide you a comprehensive package which includes free travel,
11	subsidised accommodation and a generous local salary. If you would like to
12	receive a further information on working for us overseas, please do not hesitate to contact us on 020 8675 8982.

Writing Test Part Two

- Your company has received a number of complaints from staff about their working conditions.
  The Human Resources Manager has asked you to write a report about the current situation.
- Write the **report**, including the reasons for the complaints and recommendations for dealing with them.
- Write **200–250** words.

Global brands

Making brands global

Speaking

1 What foreign brands do you buy? Why?

2 Complete the table below with the following brands and industries.

Coca-Cola	Entertainment
Hewlett-Packard	Diversified
Microsoft	Semiconductors
Nokia	Computers
McDonald's	Internet service

World's top ten brands by value, 2010

	Brand name	Origin	Industry	Value ($m)
1		USA	Beverages	70,452
2	IBM	USA		64,727
3		USA	Software	60,895
4	Google	USA		43,557
5	General Electric	USA		42,808
6		USA	Food	33,578
7	Intel	USA		32,015
8		Finland	Telecoms	29,495
9	Disney	USA		28,731
10		USA	IT	26,867

Reading

3 Look at the three aspects of a brand as illustrated below. Which aspects of the following brands do you think are global?

Coca-Cola	Mars	Hertz	Nike	Barilla	Nescafé

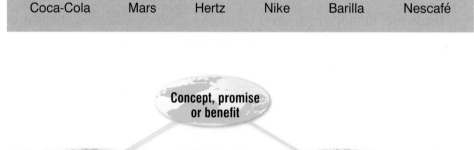

Now read the article and compare your answers.

Making brands work around the world

What are global brands and do they make sense? Jean-Noël Kapferer reports on the advantages of the global brand.

No-one disagrees with the economic necessity of geographically extending a product. Not only does it increase turnover but it also makes economies of scale possible, thus giving companies a competitive advantage in local markets. But how far do we push the global idea? Should we globalise all aspects of a brand: its name, its creative concept and the product itself?

Global branding implies the wish to extend all three aspects throughout the world. Rarely, though, is it realistic and profitable to extend all of them. The Mars brand, for example, is not absolutely global. The Mars chocolate bar is sold as an all-round nutritious snack in the UK and as an energiser in Europe (different concepts and positioning for the same physical product). Nestlé adapts the taste of its worldwide brands to local markets. The Nescafé formulas vary worldwide.

Nowhere is globalisation more desirable than in sectors that revolve around mobility, such as the car rental and airline industries. When a brand in these sectors is seen as being international, its authority and expertise are automatically accepted. Companies such as Hertz, Avis and Europcar globalised their advertising campaigns by portraying typical images such as the busy executive. An Italian businessman will identify more with a hurried businessman who is not Italian than with an Italian who is not a businessman.

The main aim of such global marketing campaigns is not to increase sales but to maximise profitability. For example, instead of bringing out different TV advertisements for each country, a firm can use a single film for one region. The McCann-Erikson agency is proud of the fact that it has saved Coca-Cola $90m over the past 20 years by producing commercials with global appeal.

Social and cultural developments provide a favourable platform for globalisation. When young people no longer identify with long-established local values, they seek new models on which to build their identity. They are then open to influence from abroad. When drinking Coca-Cola, we all drink the American myth – fresh, young, dynamic, powerful, all-American images. Nike tells young people everywhere to surpass themselves, to transcend the confines of their race and culture.

Globalisation is also made easier when a brand is built around a cultural stereotype. AEG, Bosch, Siemens, Mercedes and BMW rest secure on the 'Made in Germany' model, which opens up the global market since the stereotype goes beyond national boundaries. People everywhere associate the stereotype with robust performance.

Barilla is another example: it is built on the classic Italian image of tomato sauce, pasta, a carefree way of life, songs and sun. IKEA furniture epitomises Sweden. Lancôme expresses the sophistication of the French woman.

Certain organisational factors ease the shift to a global brand. American firms, for instance, are naturally geared towards globalisation because marketing in their huge domestic market already treats America as a single entity despite its social and cultural differences.

Another organisational factor concerns the way US companies first expanded in Europe. Many set up European headquarters, usually based in Brussels or London. From early on Europe was considered a single and homogeneous area.

Finally, a single centre of production is also a great advantage. Procter & Gamble centralises European production of detergents in its Amiens factory. This maximises product standardisation and enables innovations to spread to all countries at once, thus giving the company a competitive advantage over local rivals and ensuring the continued growth and success of the brand.

Adapted from the *Financial Times*

4 **Read the article again and choose one letter for the correct answer.**

1 To globalise a brand successfully, it is essential to
  A globalise the product, its name, logo and concept.
  B choose which parts of the brand need globalising.
  C adapt the product to local market requirements.
  D select a brand connected with international travel.

2 Companies such as Hertz globalise their advertisements by using
  A national character types.
  B successful executives.
  C Italian businessmen.
  D universal stereotypes.

3 What is the main aim of global marketing campaigns?
  A to improve margins
  B to maximise turnover
  C to cut advertising costs
  D to increase product appeal

4 Young people are a good target for globalised products because they
  A have a great deal of spending power.
  B distance themselves from traditional ideas.
  C are easily influenced by advertising.
  D want to live an Americanised lifestyle.

5 Cultural stereotypes can help globalise a product when the
  A customers like the nationality of the stereotype.
  B culture is known for high production standards.
  C associations match the type of product.
  D target market is a cosmopolitan culture.

6 Why have American companies been so successful at globalisation?
  A They are good at adapting products to local tastes.
  B They choose good locations for European headquarters.
  C They are accustomed to selling to a large diverse market.
  D They always centralise production at a single factory.

Language **5 Look at the word order in the following sentence. What do you notice about it? Find further examples of this pattern in the article and discuss how it is used.**

*Not only **does it increase** turnover but it also makes economies of scale possible.*

Speaking **6 Think of an internationally-known brand from your country which makes use of cultural stereotypes. What are the values associated with the stereotypes?**

Promoting a brand

Speaking **1** Have you bought any of these companies' products? Why/why not?

2 Choose one of the companies. How does it promote its brands in your country? Discuss the following.

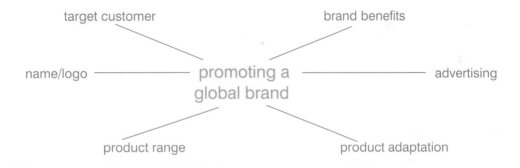

Now give a brief summary of your ideas.

3 Talk about one of the following topics for one minute.

1.40–142

- the importance of a global presence
- how to promote an imported brand
- the importance of stereotypes in advertising

Writing **4** Think of a successful domestic brand in your country. Write a 200–250 word proposal on how the brand could be globalised.

Optional task **5** Visit the Ford website at www.ford.com. Prepare a short presentation on the company's brands and markets.

Global sourcing

Choosing a supplier

Speaking

1 What types of supplier does your company use? What criteria does your company apply when choosing suppliers?

2 Companies tend to consider four main criteria when choosing a supplier. Complete the table below with the following measurements.

Per cent defective $ per unit

Satisfaction surveys   Number of new product launches a year

Time to market   Total number of days late

Warranty dollars spent   Number of items in the catalogue

Main criteria when choosing a supplier		
Criteria	**Definitions**	**Measurements**
Cost	Cost relative to our competitors	
Quality	Conformance to standards Performance Reliability	*Per cent defective*
Delivery	Speed Reliability	
Flexibility	Product range New product introduction	

3 Think of a supplier to your company. What are its strengths and weaknesses?

Supplier relationships

1 Craig Barksdale, a consultant at Jefferson Watson, talks about different types of supplier relationship. Listen and choose one letter for the correct answer.

1 Global sourcing has become so widespread because of the increasing
   A number of international mergers.
   B competitiveness of foreign markets.
   C efficiency of global communications.

2 What is the main attraction of global sourcing?
   A access to overseas markets
   B increased profit margins
   C quicker delivery times

*Craig Barksdale, consultant
Jefferson Watson*

3 What is the most common mistake companies make when sourcing globally?
   A They fail to consider all their important objectives.
   B They ignore the effect it might have on their image.
   C They forget to allow for exchange rate fluctuations.

4 When deciding on criteria for choosing a supplier, managers should
   A insist on consistently outstanding performance.
   B list and prioritise all their main objectives.
   C be as flexible as possible with their criteria.

5 What is the most important decision once a partner is selected?
   A how long-term the relationship should be
   B how the arrangement should be structured
   C how any information should be shared

6 What is the main advantage of 'buying the market'?
   A Little interaction is needed with suppliers.
   B Bidding process times are a lot quicker.
   C Administration costs are greatly reduced.

7 Strategic alliances make sense when
   A components are mutually dependent.
   B projects have a high level of financial risk.
   C development programmes are long-term.

8 Ownership of the supplier is preferable when
   A a company relies heavily on overseas suppliers.
   B cost savings are the most important factor.
   C access to vital resources is variable.

Speaking **2 What would be the most suitable type of supplier relationship in the following situations? Would it make sense for these companies to source globally?**

- a car manufacturer sourcing a brake system
- a toy company sourcing a range of plastic dolls
- a restaurant sourcing its food supplies

Global sourcing

1 **QuayWest, a European clothing company, has shortlisted five suppliers for its new range of leisurewear. Match each of the following statements with a company below. Then give each supplier a rating (from 1 to 5) for price, quality, delivery and flexibility.**

1 This supplier is able to offer a wide range of products.
2 There is a lot of old machinery in this supplier's factory.
3 This supplier is able to manufacture to the highest standards.
4 Orders are delivered extremely quickly by this supplier.
5 This supplier is hoping to improve its delivery times in the near future.
6 Doing business with this supplier could harm the company's reputation.
7 This supplier would be unable to adapt its product lines quickly.
8 This is the best supplier in terms of the relationship between price and quality.

Consort Trading Co. Ltd.
Yungtong-Dong 968, Korea

By far the most reasonably priced of the potential suppliers, this medium-sized company exports to many countries in Asia, the Pacific Rim and Europe. The company is well-established and employs a large but poorly paid workforce. This, along with obvious lack of investment in new plant, probably explains how the company is able to produce at such exceptionally low costs. These factors, however, also account for the modest quality of the goods, some of which could even fail to meet European standards. It seems that the supplier would be in a position to deliver within satisfactory times and the owners insist that they would be flexible enough to deal with last-minute orders. However, a supplier relationship with this company could possibly have serious PR implications.

Price............... Quality ....Delivery ....Flexibility ....

Samokovska, Inc.
Plodiv 4003, Bulgaria

This small but very modern company has been supplying EU countries for several years now. This experience shows in the level of workmanship and has resulted in the company adopting a policy of ensuring that each item within its catalogue conforms to all EU specifications. However, the variety of the catalogue is somewhat limited – as is the company's production capacity. It appears the company has decided on a strategy of offering an exclusive selection of high-quality, expensive products. It seems unlikely that the company would be versatile enough to respond quickly enough to market changes or deal with orders at short notice. Moreover, although the delivery times are quite impressive, the company would struggle to maintain these when faced with larger orders.

Price............... Quality ....Delivery ....Flexibility ....

Namlong

The Namlong Sportswear Company Ltd.
Bangkok 10150, Thailand

One of the largest textile suppliers in Thailand, the Namlong Sportswear Company is a large enterprise with several factories in the Bangkok area. The company employs a large workforce and relies extensively on manual labour. However, the scale of its resources means it is very flexible and its production cycles are relatively short, even for large orders. These factors, along with impressive distribution, allow the company to respond to any changes in order specifications or schedules while meeting tight deadlines. There may be some room for negotiation on prices, which look relatively expensive compared to many of Namlong's competitors in the area, especially when the slightly disappointing standard of workmanship is taken into account.

Price............... Quality ....Delivery ....Flexibility ....

Shiva Trading Co. Ltd.
Mumbai 400034, India

The Shiva Trading Company is a small but well-established family-owned business that has been exporting throughout the sub-continent and is now looking to enter the European market. To help with this expansion, it is offering very reasonable prices to potential European customers, especially in relation to the satisfactory levels of quality that its products display. On the other hand, its present size and limited capacity could lead to delays and a certain amount of inflexibility in terms of schedules and short notice orders. However, the owners insist that planned expansion of the premises will ease these pressures by increasing capacity and reducing production cycles, thus enabling the company to turn orders around more efficiently.

Price .... Quality .... Delivery .... Flexibility ....

Hai Xin Group Co. Ltd.
Shanghai 200051, China

This dynamic young company is looking for sales outlets in Europe. Although its goods tend to be slightly pricey, their quality is acceptable, with some evidence of attention to detail. However, it is not clear as yet whether these goods will conform to all EU regulations. The owners are confident, though, that their modern machinery and flexible production processes mean that the company will be able to cope with any changes in product specifications and garment features necessary to meet legal requirements. This flexibility also means that the company has already built up an impressively varied catalogue, with many items offering optional and additional features. This would suggest that introducing new product lines would not be a problem. Hai Xin also appears able to offer satisfactory delivery times.

Price .... Quality .... Delivery .... Flexibility ....

Speaking

2 **You work in the QuayWest Purchasing Department. Discuss and decide the following.**

- your key criteria for suppliers of the new range of leisurewear
- which of the five suppliers would be the most suitable

Writing

3 **Write a 200–250 word report recommending the most suitable supplier for QuayWest and giving reasons for your decision.**

1 Complete the sentences with the correct form of the following words.

> universe   adaptation   profit   advertisement
> globe   culture   diversity   product

1 Coca-Cola's marketing campaigns always transcend _____ differences.

2 Companies no longer have to develop different _____ campaigns for different countries.

3 To begin with, a company has to decide whether or not to _____ all aspects of the brand.

4 Nestlé _____ the taste of its Nescafé brand to local tastes.

5 A single centre of _____ can give a company an important competitive advantage.

6 The aim is to develop products which are _____ appealing to different nationalities and cultures.

7 Brands such as Nike are popular in such _____ markets as China and the USA.

8 To market a product _____ , companies often choose to use a global campaign.

2 Complete each sentence with a suitable preposition.

1 Young people find it easy to identify _____ the images portrayed by companies such as Nike.

2 American companies seem to be naturally geared _____ globalisation.

3 Food products are often associated _____ stereotypes from their country of origin.

4 Today's customers are accustomed _____ buying products from all over the world.

5 Many brands are built _____ the use of national stereotypes in their advertising.

6 Most American companies have traditionally treated the whole of Europe _____ a single market.

7 It is difficult to get people to distance themselves _____ local products and cultural values.

3 Match the words with a similar meaning.

1 global   traditional
2 busy   worldwide
3 essential   diverse
4 domestic   hurried
5 cosmopolitan   vital
6 robust   advantageous
7 classic   national
8 beneficial   strong

4 The graph shows the share prices for Serabi and Shanta Gold, February–May 2011. Write a 120–140 word report describing and comparing the share prices.

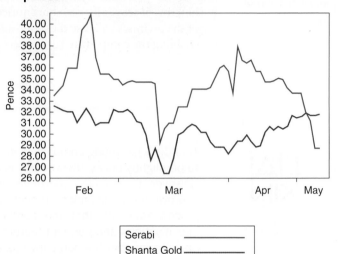

> Serabi   _____
> Shanta Gold _____

5 Match the words as they appear in the unit.

1 national   campaign
2 spending   stereotype
3 target   presence
4 global   power
5 creative   market
6 marketing   concept

Inversion

6 Rewrite the sentences beginning with the prompts.

1 We vary both the product and the way it's marketed. *Not only do we vary the product but also the way it is marketed.*

2 Our advertisements aren't usually translated.
Rarely _____
_____

3 It's easier than ever before to advertise globally.
Never _____
_____

4 Cultural differences should never be ignored.
On no account _____
_____

5 We've only had any success with it in Europe.
Only _____
_____

6 Whatever we do, we shouldn't change the logo.
Under no circumstances _____
_____

1 Choose the correct word to fill each gap.

'Buying the market' is an arrangement whereby companies publish component **(1)** _____ and ask pre-qualified vendors to bid for the contract. It is a short-term deal with almost no **(2)** _____ with the supplier and the length of the bidding process is **(3)** _____ by half. Furthermore, the cost of order **(4)** _____ falls to around $5 an order as **(5)** _____ to $50 when it is done on paper. For companies such as aircraft manufacturer Boeing, **(6)** _____ , such an arrangement with its engine suppliers would be unsuitable because of the complex **(7)** _____ between the body of the aircraft and its engines. For companies like Boeing, strategic **(8)** _____ make far more sense because they allow the company to work **(9)** _____ with its supplier, developing the aircraft's engines together. An added **(10)** _____ of this collaboration is that it reduces the financial risks of development programmes.

1 **A** standards   **B** specifications **C** criteria
2 **A** exchange   **B** feedback   **C** communication
3 **A** decreased   **B** reduced   **C** limited
4 **A** processing   **B** developing   **C** delivering
5 **A** contrary   **B** opposed   **C** different
6 **A** although   **B** nevertheless   **C** however
7 **A** structure   **B** interaction   **C** collaboration
8 **A** relationships **B** alliances   **C** arrangements
9 **A** closely   **B** precisely   **C** mutually
10 **A** potential   **B** satisfaction   **C** benefit

2 Would you use each of the following suppliers?

1 Using this supplier is unlikely to enhance our image.
2 It's uncertain whether they'll conform to standards.
3 Recent changes have lengthened production cycles.
4 The company has a comprehensive catalogue.
5 Their standard of workmanship is encouraging.
6 Exchange rates would be a factor with this supplier.
7 They fulfil our key selection criteria.
8 Short notice orders might cause potential complications.

3 Match the words with a similar meaning.

1 specification   buildings
2 warranty   measurement
3 attraction   machinery
4 reputation   guarantee
5 plant   incentive
6 premises   image

4 The graph shows unemployment in Italy and Germany, 1993–1998. Write a 120–140 word report comparing unemployment in the two countries.

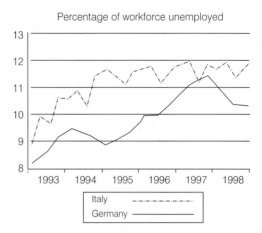

Percentage of workforce unemployed

Italy   - - - - - - - -
Germany   ——————

Grammar review

5 Complete the text by choosing the correct options.

An unexpectedly high number of high-profile boardroom changes (**1** *were confirmed/have been confirmed*) by industrial chemicals giant Chemin last week. In addition, the company announced a major reorganisation of (**2** *it's/its*) management structure after the collapse of merger talks with Paintcom, one of (**3** *the/that*) country's largest chemicals companies. Chemin failed (**4** *to win/winning*) support from its shareholders, (**5** *who/which*), according to a company spokesman, (**6** *have been holding out/ had been holding out*) right up until the deadline last Monday in the hope of a higher offer.

If the merger (**7** *would have taken place/had taken place*), the deal (**8** *would create/would have created*) the country's largest chemicals company. Although the company (**9** *will not be releasing/will not have released*) details of the planned restructuring until next week at the earliest, the plans (**10** *are likely to/ are set to*) involve the disposal of a large proportion of Chemin's assets.

Rumours of several hundred redundancies at Head Office (**11** *also circulated/have also been circulating*) since the company (**12** *announced/has announced*) that a major reorganisation (**13** *will be/would be*) necessary. Not only (**14** *cutbacks are feared/are cutbacks feared*) in the industrial solvents division, but there are also concerns about radical restructuring of the French polishing division. A company spokesman said that staff will be the first to be informed of any reductions as soon as decisions (**15** *are made/will be made*).

Listening Test Part One (2.04)

- You will hear a sales executive presenting a computer system for electronic meetings.
- As you listen, for questions **1–12**, complete the notes using up to **three** words or a number.
- You will hear the recording twice.

DecisionMaker® – Solutions for Electronic Meetings

What is DecisionMaker®?

1 DecisionMaker® allows you to hold electronic meetings on _____ .

2 Using computers enables people to express ideas freely without _____ .

Advantages of DecisionMaker®

3 The system generates more ideas by using the _____ of the entire group.

4 The system encourages _____ by keeping the proposer's identity secret.

5 Each idea is judged _____ rather than attitudes towards the proposer.

6 As a result of this team ownership of any proposals made, ideas are _____ , allowing them to be processed more quickly.

7 Equal contributions mean _____ of the meeting by individuals.

8 Automatic documentation means a _____ is not required.

Features of DecisionMaker®

9 The Whiteboard® means that _____ are accessible to the group.

10 FileShare® allows for the _____ within the group.

11 Consensus® offers three possible _____ for indicating opinions.

12 Briefcase® allows you to use your _____ in the meeting.

Listening Test Part Two (2.05)

- You will hear five different people talking about their jobs.
- For each extract there are two tasks. For Task One, choose the department each speaker works in from the list **A–H**. For Task Two, choose the complaint each speaker makes about a colleague from the list **I–P**.
- You will hear the recording twice.

TASK ONE – DEPARTMENT

- For questions **13–17**, match the extracts with the departments, listed **A–H**.
- For each extract, choose the department each speaker works in.
- Write **one** letter **A–H** next to the number of the extract.

13 .....

14 .....

15 .....

16 .....

17 .....

A legal

B sales

C accounts

D purchasing

E customer service

F despatch

G production

H personnel

TASK TWO – COMPLAINT

- For questions **18–22**, match the extracts with the complaints, listed **I–P**.
- For each extract, choose the speaker's main complaint about a colleague.
- Write **one** letter **I–P** next to the number of the extract.

18 .....

19 .....

20 .....

21 .....

22 .....

I constant interruptions

J personal telephone calls

K untidiness in the office

L bad time-keeping

M frequent breaks

N food in the office

O gossiping about staff

P misuse of office equipment

Listening Test Part Three (2.06)

- You will hear an interview with an HR director about the introduction of a new flexible working scheme.
- For each question **23–30**, mark **one** letter **A**, **B** or **C** for the correct answer.
- You will hear the recording twice.

23 The main reason why ZSV introduced the flexible working scheme was

   A to cope with social changes.

   B to respond to market forces.

   C to integrate new employees.

24 What is the main advantage of the scheme for ZSV?

   A keeping existing staff

   B recruiting new employees

   C reducing the training bill

25 Most staff join the scheme to dedicate more time to their

   A children.

   B hobbies.

   C education.

26 The old scheme was only available to

   A female workers.

   B non-managerial staff.

   C long-term employees.

27 Sally thinks the most popular element of the scheme will be

   A flexible hours.

   B job-sharing.

   C extended leave.

28 Most teleworkers keep in contact by using

   A email facilities.

   B the telephone.

   C video-conferencing.

29 What do managers find most difficult?

   A delegating work

   B keeping motivated

   C managing time

30 Employees are selected for teleworking after an assessment of their

   A home environment.

   B job description.

   C personal qualities.

Reading Test Part Four

- Read the article below about foreign language skills.
- Choose the best word to fill each gap.
- For each question **1–10**, mark **one** letter **A**, **B**, **C** or **D**.
- There is an example at the beginning (**0**).

UK comes bottom of European language league

The United Kingdom has the poorest language skills base in Europe, according to research findings published today. A European Union (**0**) ..... found that UK companies could be losing billions of pounds worth of (**1**) ..... exports due to their poor foreign language skills. Nearly twice as many UK companies (**2**) ..... experiencing difficulties due to language barriers as other European companies. Furthermore, one in eight UK companies thought they had probably missed out on a business (**3**) ..... due to their inability to communicate effectively in an international (**4**) ..... . According to the report, 'Failure to communicate effectively and efficiently with (**5**) ..... export markets in Europe, Latin America and the Asia Pacific region means that for many British firms more than a quarter of their possible revenues are at risk'.

The UK was (**6**) ..... last in a European league table, with only 74 per cent of companies saying they had employees with foreign language skills, compared with 89 per cent in Germany and 84 per cent in France. This is of particular (**7**) ..... to UK exporters, who now ship less than 25 per cent of their total (**8**) ..... to traditionally English-speaking markets. A Government spokesman said that new (**9**) ..... were needed to encourage companies to develop their language skills. 'Many companies come away from negotiations convinced that they have secured a good deal with an overseas client only to find out that the (**10**) ..... they thought they had agreed on are not as profitable as they had hoped.'

Example

0 A study   **B** examination   **C** inspection   **D** enquiry

A	B	C	D
▬	☐	☐	☐

1	**A** likely	**B**	feasible	**C**	potential	**D**	conceivable
2	**A** announced	**B**	accounted	**C**	informed	**D**	reported
3	**A** favour	**B**	opportunity	**C**	chance	**D**	fortune
4	**A** scene	**B**	neighbourhood	**C**	environment	**D**	atmosphere
5	**A** lucrative	**B**	fertile	**C**	beneficial	**D**	fruitful
6	**A** ranked	**B**	classed	**C**	graded	**D**	listed
7	**A** distress	**B**	anxiety	**C**	worry	**D**	concern
8	**A** commodities	**B**	holdings	**C**	goods	**D**	assets
9	**A** ambitions	**B**	enterprises	**C**	ventures	**D**	initiatives
10	**A** specifications	**B**	terms	**C**	conclusions	**D**	clauses

Audioscripts

Unit 1a: Work roles

Listening (1.01–1.05)

I've just moved from a company with a very strict hierarchy to a fast-growing software company and it's been hard coming to terms with the changes. I mean, don't get me wrong, I enjoy my new job a lot more. I have a lot more responsibility now and everything's done in project teams and managed by objectives. The one thing I do miss, however, is that now, once a project's running, the team's pretty much on its own and left to solve any problems by itself. Before, there was always a superior I could turn to for help, and to be honest, I'd be much happier if that were still the case. Especially when you're starting a new job, having someone to talk to can make things a lot easier.

I produce technical documents, you know, users' manuals and that sort of thing – nothing creative, I'm afraid. Our team's responsible for its own work schedules. And as long as everything's finished before the machine's shipped, it's up to us when we do it. So you'd think with email and everything, we'd all be able to work from home or come and go as we please – but that's not the case. Unfortunately, it's a very conservative company so everyone's still clocking in and out at the same time. I suppose the managers have always worked a routine nine to five and just can't imagine anything else being possible.

I'm an IT consultant and I'm working for a small leisure group on a one-year contract. So I'm travelling around Europe a lot, which I know sounds very glamorous, but it's just a case of jetting in, fixing a hotel's computer and then jetting out again. It also means I'm on call and work very ... shall we say 'flexible' hours, including many weekends. Oh and I'm also responsible for the website, which I work on from home. What I miss is support from colleagues, you know, being able to discuss problems or things like the latest technology with other IT professionals in the same job. So, yes, it's definitely the social side of my job I'd like to improve.

Well, I'm a temp and I'm working as a PA for a law firm in London just now. It's a medium-sized firm that's grown quickly so its organisation is very much like that of a smaller company. OK, I know it's unreasonable to expect a definite job description – I mean, if something needs doing, then I think whoever's available should do it. But I'm already responsible for managing the diaries and correspondence of two senior managers, so when the telephone's ringing all day and people keep asking me to photocopy reports or even make them coffee, it just becomes impossible to get anything done.

I work for the UK subsidiary of a Japanese company and it's very Japanese in terms of the way it's run. I've just got a new boss, who's come over from Japan. We seem to be getting on pretty well at the moment – he always has time for me and gives me lots of support. The only thing is, I don't really have a huge say in what I do – which is all right but sometimes it would be nice to be able to show a bit of initiative. Our work processes are totally standardised as fixed routines, which I don't mind. It's just that I always have to consult him before I can make even the smallest alteration to any job of any sort.

Unit 1b: Company structure

Listening

I = Interviewer   D = Don

I   So, what effect do you expect the change to retirement age to have on businesses?

D   Well, we have had a reasonable degree of flexibility in retirement age for a long time now. Several years ago we changed our company policy so that employees could stay on at work beyond the age of 65, if they were men or 60 for women, as long as the employer agreed that they could. Some people, of course, choose to retire and others prefer to take retirement earlier. So, in one sense, these changes are likely to have little effect. Those people who want to continue working will probably do so. Those who wish to retire will. Where it affects businesses is in the administration of people's retirement, and in cases where an employee wants to continue working, but the employer thinks otherwise.

I   And how many people do you think this will affect?

D   It is difficult to put an exact figure on it. Our research showed that the overwhelming majority of requests to continue working were accepted: 81 per cent of them to be precise. So it is only in a minority of cases that someone will want to continue working, but the company would prefer for them not to. It's in these cases where we will have to find new roles or new responsibilities.

I   Will this have any impact on company structure, do you think?

D   This is where the difficulty lies, and where companies are most likely to encounter problems. We already have an aging working population, and younger employees are not getting the opportunities in their careers.

I   You mean they are being passed over for promotion?

D   It's more than that; it's a matter of younger employees getting the experience they need to succeed their elders when they eventually give way and retire. In a tight labour market, any company would want to retain highly skilled and experienced staff. And in many ways it makes sense for them to keep senior, more experienced people on for longer, even beyond retirement age, if they can. However, this means that staff have been missing out on gaining the experience that their older colleagues have. What you have is a company that is top heavy in people in their 60s or even 70s. This, in turn means that people in their 30s or 40s have been looking elsewhere for the career development that they require.

I   And how is that likely to impact on the culture of companies?

D   Naturally, every different company will deal with this problem in their own way. I expect that most will find a pretty similar solution. One way forward is for companies to retain people beyond the age of 65, but in a role which will encourage development of expertise. We started looking at this as a possible solution last year.

I   You mean companies are likely to redeploy experienced people in a training role?

D   I don't think it will be as formal as that – I'm not talking about specific training for people who already have the skills that enable them to do their jobs well. I would expect more experienced people working alongside younger staff, in a mentoring role, passing on the kind knowledge that can only come from experience. One can imagine, for example, an experienced engineer working alongside a younger colleague. The training that has already started is proving to be successful as older engineers have been gradually handing over decision making to their younger colleagues.

I   Then you don't see older employees taking on new roles or adapting to changes in the company?

D   I wouldn't say that. I can't see any reason why older staff shouldn't be able to adapt. There has been some reluctance on the part of individuals. I see this as a personal, rather than an employment problem. We see it as a staff solution to a problem, rather than a division among our employees. Change is something that affects all of us, experienced people as well as newer people.

I   And how about in the workplace? How do you help older workers to take new ideas on board?

D   I think this is the greatest challenge that employers face and is where the greatest benefits will be found. One thing that all businesses, large, small and medium-sized will have to do is to accept that the workforce dynamic will change. In my company and many others like it – competitors and those operating in other market sectors as well as in other industries – we are looking for ways of making greater use of the increased diversity that will come into the workforce. We have to develop teams of workers on the shop floor, for example, where we look to the balance of youth and experience. We have already developed teams, where younger staff have more formal qualifications and older people have greater experience.

I   And how have people adapted to working in these teams?

D   Very well, on the whole. We had expected managers and team leaders to take on the responsibility of resolving conflict and building mutual respect. What we've found is this has happened organically, with hardly any intervention from outside the teams. People accepted the changes quite readily and learned new skills from each other. There is an increased dynamism that has developed. The young have been acquiring the working habits of their older colleagues. Absenteeism has decreased and new ideas and practices are becoming more easily accepted. I think this was all because of how we organised people into teams. Out first thought was about the people, not the job or any implications for productivity. We allowed people to make their own decisions about how they worked, and our staff made good use of that opportunity.

I   How do you see this developing in the future?

D   What I hope we will be able to do is take what we have learned from this and adapt it to other changes in the workplace. We're moving into an era of increased flexibility in the workforce, with such things as teleworking and hot-desking becoming the norm. As long as we can encourage our people to work in diverse teams – not only age related, I'm thinking of multi-skilled teams as well – then I can see teams operating as skill-sharing units within the company. I believe this can only be good for motivation and so for productivity, too. I think this is the challenge we have to rise to in the future.

Unit 2a: Stocks and shares

Listening 1 1.07

ex 1 - language

R = Richard   K = Katie

R   Now retail stocks. They were quite strong about a year ago, but they have been quite volatile recently. So the question is, has the financial crisis driven them down? Our retail correspondent Katie Johnson joins me in the studio. So, Katie, first of all what drove these prices up in the first place?

K   Well, some of the news stories about increased growth and the competition for market share would have attracted some investors looking for a quick profit – but I think the real driving force has been the fact that demand has exceeded supply. It has always been thought that retailers would do well in bad as well as good times. And during the consumer boom of the last few years, there was a noticeable shift towards reliable stocks, and with few share offers and a general unwillingness to sell, prices rose.

R   And this is all because retailers were seen as a safe investment?

K   Generally speaking, yes. When consumers have money to spend, they spend it and retailers are only too happy to provide the luxury items they want.

R   And what about good old profits? Did they match the performance of the share price?

K   Well, that's the interesting thing. As more and more consumers were busily spending, so retailers' profits went up. Much of that profit was reinvested, back into the businesses, as retailers looked for increased share of what was thought to be an ever expanding market. Take Tesco, for example. They are probably the most successful of the food retailers over the last ten years or so. Then, they had about a 25 per cent share of the grocery market. Today it is more than 30 per cent.

R   So everyone wants to invest in the bigger players in the game?

K   There is another reason, too. As a retailer, Tesco have been around for a long time, and were a well known store throughout the UK, even before they came to dominate the marketplace. What is interesting is the change in its position in the market that Tesco has undergone. They were originally a shop where people went to buy food cheaply. Tesco's recent history has been one of expansion in the UK and overseas, and one of diversification. They now sell groceries alongside white goods, financial services and clothing, to name but a few. Other retailers have followed suit, but Tesco has led the way. Throughout the boom, it seemed that everything Tesco touched would turn to gold. Investors are always looking to a business they know, even if their position changes.

R   As long as it remains successful, though?

K   Naturally. Unless there is a return, the investors will look elsewhere.

R   And grocery retailers have remained successful, haven't they?

K   In the main, yes. The big fish have continued to lead the sector, but it hasn't been easy. Tesco, and the other leading chains came under pressure from new players, such as Lidl and Aldi. These retailers came in at the discount end of the market. And while their share remains relatively small, some two or three percent, they have made inroads into Tesco's share – that fell by half of one percent over the last couple of years.

R   So, let's turn to the effect of the financial crisis. How has that affected the larger retailers?

K   Well, the immediate effect on consumers was one that shook their confidence. We all saw the TV pictures of giant financial institutions going to the wall, of bank employees walking out of their offices with their personal effects in boxes and for a time none of us knew where it would end. This shock made people very uncertain, and they suddenly became much more careful with their disposable income. Confidence in the stock markets fell, too. We were due a sell-off of highly valued shares. Investors took their profits and looked for safer places taking a more long term view of what they were prepared to invest. Some of those profits went into the bond market, and some into precious metals.

R   For many people the fall in share prices seems surprising. Recession or no recession, people still need to buy food. So, why did share prices fall?

K   The simple answer is the usual one. Confidence. As I hinted at before, investors saw the overall falls following the bank collapses and moved to more long term investments. It's no accident that the price of gold has risen to record levels in recent months. Another reason is that the big grocers are no longer simply food retailers. Tesco, for example, sells 16 per cent of all microwave ovens in the UK and has significant interests in telecoms and insurance. When consumers are forced to tighten their belts, it's the large ticket items – the expensive goods – that are the first that they cut back on.

R   So there is likely to be a downward trend in share price, then?

K   Yes and no. There was an appreciable fall throughout the markets in the initial wake of the bank collapses; a rationalisation of the market as it appeared to be at the time. Then share prices levelled out, although there are still challenges that these companies need to face up to – from competitors and from changes in consumer spending. There are still profits to be made, still rises and falls depending on local conditions but in the short to medium term we can expect some stability overall.

R   OK, then Katie, here's the big question. What's the market going to do next?

K   Oh, now, Richard, that's not easy to say with any certainty at all. The prices being paid will, inevitably, reflect the value of the company – as the market sees it, if not in real terms, and we are talking about high value businesses here. I can't see share prices falling for ever, and there is evidence that the prices have bottomed out and even begun to climb back. They are not yet at the levels they were at before the crisis, but moving in that direction. I think we can look forward to some interesting times. Once the discount sellers are better established in the market, they might think about repositioning themselves, just as Tesco did, and then the competition will regain some of its old edge. On the other hand, it may be that the market leaders will look to consolidate their core businesses, before going on to even bigger ventures. I think the wise investor can look forward to substantial returns, but they may take some time to be made.

Listening 2 1.08

R   Now earlier you talked about Tesco, the UK's largest supermarket chain. And I understand you have a graph illustrating what's been happening to their share price over the last three months.

K   Yes, and here it is. Now this is more or less typical of what's been happening throughout the sector for the last year, although Tesco being Tesco have been in a position to make themselves more attractive to investors than perhaps any of their competitors. The price had been reasonably stable at the end of last year. But as you can see, in the period immediately after Christmas there were some fluctuations. The price finally recovered, even reaching a high towards the end of February. But then the price fell and fell, even despite some small rises, due mainly to profit-taking from investors, I think. So that, by the middle of March the price had fallen to a low of 378, from a high of 413 three weeks previously. It then finally rallied, getting back to just over the 405 mark in April. It fell slightly, before settling back to around the 395 that it is today.

R   That's not another dip in consumer confidence bringing the price down from 413, is it?

K   No, I don't think so. We can expect a dip in spending in the months after Christmas, when not many of us have much spare cash to spend anyway. A fall in sales is fairly predictable at that time of year, and there's no suggestion of a price collapse. No, I think the reason is that those people who bought Tesco shares when they were round about 380 decided to take their profit and sell them once the price had reached 405 or thereabouts. If you had bought say 10,000 shares at £3.80 and sold them at £4.05, you would have made a tidy £2,500. Not bad for a month's investment.

Unit 2b: Mergers and acquisitions

Listening   1.09

Good morning. My name is Jason Labone and I work for Hinton and Bailey. We're an economic research consultancy, operating from the UK and we provide businesses with economic forecasting data. Today, I am here to say a little about what has been happening in mergers and acquisitions since the financial crisis of 2008. I will first look at why there has been something of an increase in the number of mergers in the last year or so and then move on to explain my view on how the recent spate of mergers differs from those that took place before the crisis and the downturn that resulted from that. Finally, I will say something of how I expect the future to develop, at least in the short to medium term. I hope to leave some time, at the end of the session for any questions or comments you may have, and perhaps we can end with some discussion of what businesses need to do to survive and to grow in the current economic circumstances.

So, why has there been an increase in the number of mergers, now that the financial sector has stabilised itself somewhat? One reason is that the recession the crisis provoked has led to a fall in profitability for many businesses in almost every industry. A further result of the recession has been that the market has changed, for many businesses. We have witnessed a sharp fall in customer confidence – spending is down and so are orders and companies are realising that long-term growth is hard to find. What's more, as a consequence of the financial crisis, share prices fell, and so a company's value has fallen, also. And while all this is going on, the financial institutions, and I am referring to the banks, here, have been rescued by governments. In many cases government has become the largest shareholder in these institutions. The banks are under pressure from government to generate finance to move the economy out of recession, and this is particularly so when the government is also a major shareholder.

Even in the financial sector itself, there has been a rash of mergers and the reasons behind these are typical of the reasons behind mergers in other sectors. Even before the financial crisis, small and medium-sized Building Societies had become less profitable. The larger players in the sector had issued shares and become banks. This enabled them to compete more effectively, and in their attempts to maintain their profits, the smaller societies overstretched themselves in new, niche markets. This was made worse by the tightening of the property market after the crisis. Still further, as the economy started to rebuild, they were faced with the increased cost of increased financial regulation. The upshot is that there have been more than twelve mergers in this sector alone since the crisis of 2008. What we have seen in the industry is a phase of re-organisation in the face of new economic realities and this is a pattern we have seen, not only in other industries, but in other economies as well.

The question is, then, how is this surge in mergers different from those that occurred in the 1990s and again in the years before the financial crisis? I have already pointed out that the banks are under pressure, from government, to make finance available in order to help lead the economy out of recession. But nowadays, banks are behaving differently to the way they were before they were bailed out. Prior to 2008, banks were willing to take greater risks in search of profit, and it was this that helped to cause many institutions to get into trouble and some to fail. Banks are no longer willing to make 'bad' loans. However, acting conservatively, banks are making credit available, but only where it makes good sense, where it will assist businesses in an industry to grow securely.

Let me give you an example; Kraft's takeover of Cadbury is typical of the current round of mergers. Before 2008, the most likely bid for Cadbury would have been from private equity, but this was not the case after the crisis. While the takeover was ongoing, there was talk of rival bids from industry rivals, such as Hershey and Nestlé. Incidentally, the same can be said for other recent mergers, too. This is reassuring for shareholders – and government is a shareholder these days. What reassures is that these mergers are seen as more sustainable, leading to long-term growth. Shareholders are pleased with the increase in value of their shares and government is happy that the industry is re-organising itself with an eye to the future. The financial institutions are able and prepared to finance deals like this because they see them as 'good' loans, enabling mergers which put the business in a better position to grow and make profit in the long term, guaranteeing that the debt will be repaid.

What then of the future? Well, we can't say that this is a trend that will continue forever, but for the present economic cycle the picture is more clear. With government as a shareholder we can expect to see the banks acting more and more conservatively in their lending. Gone are the days of the speculative takeover. We will see mergers and acquisitions funded at least partly by the banks, but with caution over the risks they are taking. We also expect to see, to a greater extent than before 2008, bidders using their own financial resources to fund mergers. Over the next few years, we shall see CEOs increasingly focused on maintaining a secure credit rating while looking for growth opportunities. At the same time, financial institutions will be looking at opportunities for less riskier, long-term credit. Having being bitten once by bad debt, the banks will want to ensure that their loans are repaid.

Unit 3b: Entering a market

Listening   1.10

So, what's it like actually doing business with the Chinese? Well, it's difficult to describe because in China there's still no commonly shared perception of what's reasonable or normal in international business, so standards and expectations vary widely from place to place. That's why, when you're doing business in China, it's imperative that you do extensive preparatory work. This means finding out about the particular company, industry, city or region where you're doing business – and not just about the country as a whole.

One of the first things to remember is that the Chinese find it most discourteous if you are late for meetings. It may be, of course, that your first meeting will be in your hotel, but if not, then allow plenty of time for the journey as in most Chinese cities the congestion is every bit as bad as in London. A good tip is to take a business card with the company's address written in Chinese to show the taxi driver. When you get there, you will be greeted by your host, usually a senior manager, and probably some of his or her staff. The visitors will then be ushered into the meeting room.

The leader of your group will be expected to enter first and will generally be offered a seat beside the most senior Chinese person present. This person will usually chair the meeting and act as host and have a translator at his or her side. To begin with, all those present will swap business cards, in itself a very important ceremony, and there will be a short period of small talk. The host will then officially start proceedings with a 'brief introduction' to the Chinese enterprise and its activities. The host may then invite the visiting team to speak. Now at this point it's appropriate for the UK side to begin to make its case. Don't forget to warn your host beforehand if you wish to include any audio-visual aids during this presentation. It's also extremely important that your team should be able to answer any questions on any aspect of your business proposal, your own company and your international competitors.

Following the meeting, the Chinese enterprise will probably arrange a special dinner for the UK guests. Small talk over dinner is essential for relationship-building. For most Chinese, the family counts above all else. It remains the dominant social and political unit in Chinese society so Chinese people will usually be very pleased to be asked about their children and their hopes for their children's future. In social relationships Chinese people almost always seek to preserve harmony and face. Hosts believe it is their duty to offer their visitors hospitality, even though the visitors themselves may much prefer a day off after intense negotiations. It's very common, for instance, for the host enterprise to organise sightseeing trips for its guests and it would, of course, be a discourtesy not to accept these invitations.

Unit 4a: The future of work

Listening 1.11

I = Interviewer   NT = Neil Traynor

I   In the late 1990s, a small property company, Cottice Holdings, opened its first multi-occupant office building in the village of Aldbourne, about 50 miles to the west of London. As office buildings go, it wasn't an expensive project. Construction costs came to a little under two million pounds. It was, however, a project filled with risk. The developers had an idea, built the complex and waited for occupants. They were in the heart of the countryside, half an hour's drive from the motorway and access to the capital. So what was the thinking behind the project? We spoke to Cottice's MD, Neil Traynor.

NT It all started out as an idea sketched out on a napkin in a restaurant. Some friends and I, who were all self-employed professionals, lived locally and worked from home, were having one of our regular meals. We'd meet up about three or four times a year to chat and compare work – networking, really. Someone came up with an idea of having a space away from home with access to all the things we had in our home offices without moving to the big city. We knew what we wanted and where we wanted it, but had no idea of how we could do it.

I   What exactly did you want to do?

NT To find, or rather create, a good place where people would want to come and work. But, when we sat down and thought about it, we realised it needed to be more than that. Many self-employed people are pretty flexible by nature, and this meant we needed to provide them with a suitable working environment to reflect this. We started out with the idea of sharing offices between us, but for one reason or another that proved impossible. We decided to rent out office space to people in all sorts of industries. We looked at parking, the size of the offices, sharing communications and things like that. One important consideration was that there could be no hierarchy among the self-employed. Here, everyone is his or her own boss. So we don't have facilities like reserved parking or executive toilets.

I   So how is the building laid out?

NT It's centred around what we originally called the Resource Area. There's a kitchen with all the usual facilities, and next to it there was a room with a photocopier for the tenants to share. But in a relatively short space of time, we realised this was unnecessary. Technology had moved on and people were able to use their PCs to print copies of whatever they needed. What the tenants wanted was a space to sit, relax and look at the newspapers. So that's now a lounge area. We've recently added a TV, so people can catch up with the news that way, too. That's on the first floor, along with three of the smaller offices. Below that, on the ground floor, is the reception area and the two large offices. The top floor has five more offices. That makes ten in all. They're all connected by a central stairway. People tend to bump into each other in the corridors, and then socialize in the lounge.

I   So people meet by chance, rather than intentionally, then?

NT At first, yes. Remember the people in these offices don't work together. Each office is actually a separate business. What we've tried to create is an organic space for people to use as they wish; and I think we've succeeded in this. The lounge itself was established because the tenants asked for it. They wanted a place where they could sit and chat with other workers in the building. The reception area is an important focal point, too. We have a picture gallery of the tenants there. This helps to let them know who is a part of the office community, and it helps with security too. It's good for people to know who comes and goes from the building. The reception desk isn't staffed full time, and the tenants have begun to keep an eye on the area, informally throughout the day. Having a central rest area has really helped this community feeling to grow.

I   Do you think that these offices have made a difference to the way people work?

NT In some ways, yes. In others, no. Work is work and all our tenants are hard working, self-motivated people, who like to get on with things. However, they do find it easier to be more productive away from the home environment. They definitely step into "work" when they arrive here. I also think that one thing self-employed people sometimes find difficult is the lack of day-to-day interaction with colleagues. People often use the lounge as a place to talk through ideas or problems, and they are generally doing this with a colleague who works in an entirely different field. It's changed the way we look at the office, too. We're planning another development, not too far from here. We're paying much more attention to how we can foster the sense of community that we enjoy here. What we've realised is that people need contact with the people they share a building with, just as much as they need the work that they do.

I   Even when your tenants are all self-employed in different fields?

NT Yes. There is an enormous amount of everybody's work which is similar to, or related to the work someone else in another field does. Among the people in this building are a couple of accountants, a designer and several people in financial services. We've also seen tenants whose businesses have outgrown these offices. The self-employed have become employers and have moved on to larger premises. Much of business is about networking, and I know that John, one of the accountants does some work for one of our former tenants who has moved on to bigger and better things. That's just one of the many contacts that have come from the shared workplace. We're looking into ways that we can connect our new site with this one, precisely for that reason. Contact, it seems, has become our selling point.

Unit 4b: e-business

Listening 1.12–1.16

Well, it's already made a huge impact and by the time the project's fully implemented, we'll have networked over 300,000 employees and suppliers – they'll all be able to communicate through email. And it's this interconnectivity, it's changing everything about the way we work. I mean, last year around 15 per cent of our in-service staff development was carried out through Web-based distance learning using the company intranet. And we reckon that for every 1,000 days of classroom-based teaching that's supplied by distance learning, it generates about $500,000 in efficiency gains. And this year we'll be delivering up to 30 per cent of our courses by distance learning. So we'll be looking at savings of over $100 million.

We're one of the largest insurance organisations in Canada, offering a wide range of financial products. We rely on a system of independent agents to distribute our products so it's really important to maintain a close relationship with them. This used to be done over the telephone but that was all very time-consuming for our employees and meant we could only supply agents with information during office hours. Now we have the extranet, which means that all our representatives can keep in touch around the clock and get the latest information about offerings. They can also request back-up articles and information such as telemarketing scripts and advertisements. And of course, we'll be introducing more and more new product lines so it's essential that our agents get the back-up they need.

We're one of the Netherlands' leading banks with 1,300 branches here and abroad. We deal with both businesses and consumers but our primary focus is small and medium-sized businesses – SMBs as we call them. As part of our offering to SMBs, we recently launched a Web-based euro project which provides free briefings to both customers and staff about the European currency. Since the issues surrounding the euro are constantly changing, people need regular updating. By providing up-to-the-minute bulletins, we're establishing ourselves as a major player in the Eurozone countries. This, in turn, is enhancing our clients' perceptions of us and we'll be aiming to strengthen and expand our customer base in the near future.

Well, we are one of France's most prestigious bicycle manufacturers, selling mainly to professionals and people with a real passion for cycling as a sport. The best bit about our new website is that it lets customers actually design their own personalised cyber cycle. All they have to do is choose a basic model and then decide what frame, wheels, pedals, colour and so on they want. They pay online by credit card and the bike is then delivered to their nearest dealer within 14 days. It's as simple as that. Our business was initially aimed at mostly French customers but with the new way of using the internet, we have been able to create an international presence at a fraction of what it would have cost to advertise outside the domestic market.

After recent restructuring we felt we needed to change the company culture to reflect our leaner structure. Processes that used to be highly bureaucratised needed to be simplified. One area we really had to tackle was procurement. After filling in massive amounts of paperwork, getting requisite signatures and then faxing orders off, our employees sometimes had to wait over a month for things like office material and PCs to get here. A real advantage with the new system is there's less margin for error because if the form isn't filled in correctly, then the system says so immediately. So less time'll be wasted on sorting out problems. By the end of the year we'll have reduced our paper invoices from five million to zero.

Unit 4: Exam practice (Exam focus CD)

Listening Part One

Good morning and welcome to Eldertree Cosmetics. My name's Maria Darcy and I'm the Managing Director. I'm here today to tell you a little bit about the history of the company before you're taken on the official tour.

So, Eldertree Cosmetics was founded by Olivia Jenkins in 1975 originally under the name of Eldertree Cottage. And in those days it really was very much a cottage industry with Olivia and her husband Mike producing a range of natural soaps in their own kitchen. The soaps proved to be a recipe for success and sales took off due to the popularity of simple, chemical-free products. It soon became clear, though, that Olivia and Mike would be unable to satisfy demand if they continued working out of their kitchen. So in 1977 Mike began searching for suitable premises and this resulted in the move to the Old Bakery in the town centre.

At the start of the next decade sales continued to grow dramatically and Olivia and Mike widened their product range to enter new markets such as haircare and cosmetics. This led to rapid expansion and a change of name to Eldertree Cosmetics. It was at this point that Olivia and Mike realised they needed support with their sales and marketing efforts. So they took on an experienced Sales Manager, who was able to win substantial contracts with some of the largest UK cosmetics retailers.

This significant increase in business meant that Eldertree needed to recruit a lot more staff and upgrade its facilities. The company had reached a critical point. In order to develop, it required the resources and knowledge that only a large and established organisation could offer. And faced with several takeover bids, Olivia and Mike finally decided that in the interests of Eldertree and its employees, they would sell the company to the UK's biggest high-street chemist, Greenaway, which they did in 1987.

Greenaway's first move was to look at ways of increasing productivity. Although the Old Bakery site had been upgraded over the years, it was still limited by its size and layout. So in 1988 Greenaway began construction of the new factory, which was completed at the end of the following year. The other major decision which was taken at this time was to continue to trade under the Eldertree brand name and not that of its parent company.

Today Eldertree Cosmetics is a state-of-the-art producer of high-quality cosmetic products. Structural changes have seen certain functions move to Greenaway's Head Office. By moving its marketing operations to Greenaway, for example, Eldertree has not only cut costs, but also enjoyed the advantages of its parent's substantial advertising budget. And I'm sure you're all familiar with the new TV campaign. Despite the fact that Eldertree has grown enormously, it still retains a family atmosphere, with many of the original employees from the Old Bakery still working for the company today. Over the last ten years or so, these loyal employees have seen the Eldertree name successfully establish itself as a market leader in both the UK and overseas.

On that note, I'd like to hand you over to Samantha Eagle, our PR Manager, who'll be conducting your tour of the factory today.

Part Two

Well, I guess on the whole it was quite interesting talking about setting and meeting objectives and co-ordinating projects. It's just that I'd hoped we'd learn more practical things like how to motivate groups and manage conflict and make group communication more effective. Anyway, I was pretty tired by the end of the day and I got in quite late because the centre was a long way from home. But that in itself wasn't really a problem. I think one day would have been more than enough. I didn't really understand

why they needed two whole days. It wasn't that expensive though, so I'm hoping I'll be allowed to go on another course soon. There are some good writing skills courses around, I believe.

I feel a lot more confident now having done the course. The trainer gave us some really great tips on preparing more effectively. And I also got to see myself on video. There I was talking about our latest product when most of the time I was standing in front of the screen. So no-one in the audience could see my nice OHTs anyway. We certainly didn't have any complaints about the price even though it was pretty expensive. But I can't understand why they held it in Newcastle. It took me half the day to get there and I was exhausted before the course even started. We really should have found somewhere closer to the office.

I had a great time. We did lots of role-plays, mainly about delegating or dealing with interruptions, which I really enjoyed. And I think it must have done me some good. Even my boss has noticed that I'm getting better at prioritising my workload. And this week I managed to get my report in before the deadline for a change. There must have been about twenty of us by the time all the latecomers had arrived, which was about right for the group dynamics. The only thing that I'd change would be the refreshments. You'd have thought they could have provided more than just a salad for lunch, wouldn't you? It wasn't even particularly fresh either.

Originally, I'd wanted to do the effective negotiations course. But my boss told me this course would be more useful. You know what I'm like. Even when I don't want to do something, I end up saying 'yes'. Even now I still find it difficult to say 'no', but at least this course has made me more confident about trying to stick up for myself. We covered a lot of stuff. But of course you can't expect the trainer to do everything in just six sessions, can you? So we had to miss out on some really interesting topics. I was a bit disappointed, for example, that we didn't do anything on body language.

The programme itself looked really interesting, which is why I went for this course rather than the assertiveness training one. And I guess we did have a few useful topics like writing minutes and preparing agendas. And we started looking at roles, especially the role of the chairperson. But all in all, it was really disappointing and so chaotic. We never really knew what we were supposed to be doing. But then the tutor didn't seem to know either. She kept taking calls on her mobile during the sessions and I wouldn't be surprised if it was someone phoning her to tell her what to do next! Good job it didn't cost too much. Otherwise we'd have been asking the centre for our money back.

Part Three

S = Sue   P= Peter

S   And today on Business Spot we have the winner of the 'South-East Company of the year' award. Peter Jones, Manager of corporate travel agency Corporate Direct. Hello Peter. And congratulations on your award.
P   Thank you, Sue.
S   So, Peter, how has the award affected your company so far?
P   Well, Sue, we've been stunned by all the media attention, which might even generate some new business, you never know. But the real benefit is the boost to morale. Everyone's been working extremely hard to make the business a success and it's great to see their efforts rewarded.
S   So why did you start Corporate Direct?
P   Well, about six years ago I was made redundant. I couldn't really see myself working for any of the local travel agencies. And I'd always wanted to do my own thing. So I decided it was now or never.
S   What did your wife think?
P   She wasn't too keen initially. She didn't want me turning her home into a travel agency. But thankfully it wasn't long before we could open a small office.
S   And business is still booming. Some of your services are expanding very rapidly.
P   Yes, they are. Core services like car rental were popular right from the word go, although what's really taken off is our monthly journal Travel Direct. Subscriptions are increasing at ten to twenty per cent a month. We're also looking at ways of promoting our currency exchange service.
S   So things are obviously going very well for you. But what exactly makes Corporate Direct so unique?

P Well, although there are two other independent travel offices here in the area, offering people the same unbiased advice, as far as I know, we're still the only company keeping a comprehensive database of clients' travel guidelines, things like which airlines they use ...

S ... meaning you make arrangements in line with each company's policies ...

P Yes, that's right. And like the other big names, we can also provide very competitive rates too.

S And as I understand it, you've also been developing the consultancy arm of the company as well. What services do you currently offer?

P Well, advising companies on their travel policies is a very popular service and one which looks set to develop even further. What really attracts companies, though, is our corporate hospitality consultancy. We advise people on all sorts of PR type things, everything from wine-tasting to car-racing. We've also seen an increase in the number of clients asking our advice on language training courses.

S But why does a company use an agency rather than make its own arrangements? Wouldn't it be cheaper?

P Well, some companies do of course arrange things themselves. And in some cases it may indeed be cheaper for them to do so. But what's most important for companies, though, is that by using a corporate travel agency, they get everything arranged far more quickly, without the hassle of dealing with numerous providers. And I suppose our clients appreciate not having to worry about quality. Quite simply, we take the stress out of organising corporate travel.

S So, who are your biggest clients?

P Well, there's quite a range. We've got clients in the retail industry, like fashion companies, for example, and we're seeing far more interest from hotels and catering companies. Although, in general, I'd say our customers are more often than not from accountancy firms or banks and I can't see that changing in the future.

S Speaking of the future, what new ventures are planned for Corporate Direct?

P Well, we're introducing a 24-hour emergency service in the next two to three months. Clients will be able to call our Hotline for help at any time.

S I should imagine that'll be really useful.

P Well, we hope so. But our biggest priority at the moment is updating our internet site in time for the Travel Fair in a fortnight's time. Clients will be able to access our website and book services directly from our home page. We're also considering introducing a Corporate Direct Credit Card, which will let clients settle their accounts with us on a monthly basis. But let's just say that's not exactly going to happen tomorrow.

S Well, I'm afraid we'll have to finish there. Thank you Peter for talking to us today and congratulations again on your award.

Exam focus: Speaking Test contains mock interviews.
No audioscripts are provided.

Unit 5a: Staff motivation

Listening   1.17–1.21

Well, I've only been here a few months but I feel as if I've fitted in quite well so far. Everyone seems to have time to talk to me when I need help, which I really appreciate. The work's beginning to get interesting too. It's just that by now, I feel I really should be getting up to speed. Only it's a relatively new position and nobody's really spelt out what the exact scope of the job is or what my responsibilities and priorities should be. I think my line manager needs to give me a more concrete idea of what she expects me to achieve. She's back from holiday next week so maybe we could sit down together then.

Well, I get the feeling that we're starting to fall a bit behind other companies. I mean, when you look in the papers, you can't help noticing there's a bit of a gap between ourselves and the current going rate. I mean, it's not that I'm unhappy here or anything. I really like my job – it's interesting work and I think it's great that the job's so flexible. It's just that, at the end of the day, nobody likes to feel undervalued, do they? And in my position, it's not just myself I've got to think about. I've got responsibilities outside work as well.

Well, it's great to be part of a successful team. I don't think you could wish for harder-working or more dedicated colleagues. But I just sometimes think that our efforts aren't always rewarded. I know different managers have different styles but, well, everyone likes to feel appreciated, don't they? I mean, in my last job, managers always made a point of praising us when we beat our targets. One manager even used to encourage us to clap and cheer each other. And I must admit, I do miss that at times. I find praise here is sometimes a bit, shall we say, limited. It's like there's a 'That's what you're paid for' type of attitude.

I suppose, on the whole, I've got very little to complain about really. I get on with the rest of the team and that kind of thing. But there's one thing that's been on my mind for a while now. I just feel that, well, I've reached a stage where I'm capable of dealing with a lot more responsibility than I do at present. I just don't feel stretched any more. I don't feel as though I'm contributing as much as I could. It's almost as if I'm on autopilot. Things are beginning to feel a bit stale. What I need is a bit of variety, something to get my teeth into – a challenge.

Well, you're probably already aware of the fact that things aren't functioning too smoothly in Production at the moment. I don't know what other people have said but personally I think it's down to our procedures. There's no formal system for putting our ideas forward and in the past suggestions have just been ignored. I think management has to accept a lot of the responsibility. What we need to do is schedule regular meetings, which will improve the flow of information in both directions. I mean, at the moment I get more information through the shop floor grapevine than from my line manager.

Unit 5b: Recruitment

Listening 1.22

Good afternoon. My name's Dave Archer and I'm here to tell you a little bit today about how the executive search process works. Now in Europe the executive search industry is worth $10bn a year, with a lot of that business being conducted in the UK. UK recruiters basically use one of four methods: there's agency recruitment, advertising selection (which is advertising in newspapers), a combination of selection and search and, at the top-end, executive search, otherwise known as headhunting. The executive search market is particularly prevalent in areas where market growth has been driven by skills shortages in client companies who are in a constant process of change. This is particularly the case in the finance, consulting and IT sectors, for example.

There's a fairly standard operating procedure for the delivery of headhunting assignments. It begins with a client giving a headhunter exclusive instruction and a brief to fill a vacancy. The headhunter's first task is to target potential companies, then individuals within those companies, either through desk research or through extensive contact networks. The headhunter then speaks to those individuals who match the specified criteria closely and are most appropriate for the job in question.

The headhunter then meets a number of potential candidates, either at their own offices or at a neutral location. Of course, these meetings have to be arranged and held with the utmost discretion. The headhunter then puts together the curriculum vitaes and presents his findings to the client. At this meeting the client is given a shortlist of about eight candidates and selects three or four of them for interview. This number gives a good chance of a successful candidate being hired. The candidates then go through the client's own interview procedure, possibly along with other candidates that applied directly to the company in response to an advertisement. Afterwards, the headhunter gives professional advice to both sides and facilitates the offer process to make sure that the whole assignment ends with a successful hire.

As for remuneration, the headhunter will receive a proportion, usually about 30 per cent, of the first annual salary of the person appointed. When a search company has been given an exclusive instruction to fill a vacancy, payment is normally billed in three instalments: first of all a retainer, then a second instalment upon submission of the shortlist and finally, a completion fee when the appointee starts with the client.

Now the advantage of a good headhunter is that he can provide a clear understanding of the business environment, a client's activities, their strengths and weaknesses and those of their rivals. This kind of comprehensive information can only be obtained through painstaking detective work, a close relationship with the key players in the industry and an international presence.

Headhunting is considered by many to be a 'black art' at best, unethical at worst. Yet at its highest levels, search is time and cost-efficient and provides a client with commercially sensitive information which would be otherwise unavailable. It targets those people who are happy in their current position, motivated and able to consistently deliver top performance – in other words, just the people who can benefit the client's growth plans and who cannot be accessed in any other way.

Model answers to Ex 3, page 91

 (1.23) *5b One-minute talk: How to fill a key vacancy*

In order to fill a key vacancy, a company will usually follow the same standard procedure.

It will begin by producing an accurate job description of what it would like the successful candidate to do. From this, it can then produce a profile of this ideal candidate, which is a list of skills, experience, attributes and so on.

Having produced this profile, the company must then decide on the best recruitment method to capture a candidate with this profile. This might be an internal advertisement or an external advertisement in a newspaper, on the internet say, even an agency or perhaps a headhunter.

Having decided on the best recruitment method, the advertisements are then placed or the headhunter contacted and a list of candidates will be then drawn up to be put through the company's recruitment processes. This might be interviews, psychometric tests or even hand-writing analysis. This will then produce the ideal candidate for the company.

The company will then have to negotiate terms with this candidate and, hopefully, this will result in terms which are both affordable for the company and attractive enough to get the candidate they want.

 (1.24) *5b One-minute talk: The importance of having a good CV*

Well, in my opinion, you can never underestimate the importance of having a good CV.

In the majority of cases, your CV is the employer's first impression of you, your first chance to impress your potential employer, let's say. It is the essential illustration of your suitability for the job, showing how your skills and experience match your employer's requirements.

But more than that, it shows your ability to summarise, prioritise and present information effectively, essential skills in today's job market. It also shows your linguistic and communicative abilities.

Even though employers these days use a variety of selection techniques, such as analysing your handwriting, a good CV is still the single most important part of any application.

Unit 6a: Corporate culture

Listening 1 (1.25)

I = Interviewer   MD = Managing Director

I And now to IKEA. The Swedish furniture retailer has just reported a turnover of fifty-six billion Swedish kroner from its 150 stores worldwide. Now, IKEA puts its success down to corporate culture. So with me today to explain the secret of IKEA's culture is the Managing Director of IKEA UK. Good morning.

MD Good morning.

I Now is every IKEA store really exactly the same?

MD Well, in terms of culture they're pretty well uniform. Although our culture will naturally bond with the local culture to some extent, our core values such as simplicity and cost-consciousness are valid in all cultures. So we don't need to adapt the way we operate to run our stores. And as for products, although we make some minor adaptations to suit local tastes, we produce exactly the same catalogue in all twenty-eight countries.

I And where do these values originate?

MD It all goes back to Sweden in the 50s and 60s. IKEA's founder, Ingvar Kamprad, started the company at a time of democratic and social change.

I Are IKEA's values those of its founder, then?

MD Well, they have evolved over the last fifty-seven years, of course, but I think our mission statement 'A better life for the majority of people' still very much reflects the spirit of those early years. And Ingvar regularly visits IKEA stores around the world and talks to all co-workers, especially on the shop floor.

I How does IKEA cope with such diversity amongst its employees?

MD Well, funnily enough, I've been working for IKEA for fifteen years in Sweden, Italy, Canada, the USA and here in the UK and what's struck me most is how much we have in common. People may interpret certain concepts such as responsibility and freedom differently but our core values such as humbleness exist in every country.

I So, what are the advantages of such a strong corporate culture?

MD They're tremendous. For one, there's a real bond between our operations around the world. It's easy to transfer across borders because you know the values will be exactly the same. And from a marketing and positioning point of view it's very advantageous as well. But the real pay-off is that it makes IKEA unique. You can clone our products and our store concept but not our culture. It takes years to build and it has to be maintained daily.

I But how do you educate 127,000 workers?

MD We begin by making sure people understand the values. That's why the IKEA Way seminars are so vital. All managers attend them and then it's their responsibility to pass the message on. Corporate culture also figures in meetings.

I Do you use educational videos and brochures as well?

MD Videos and brochures are helpful tools but only if used in conjunction with 'walking the talk' and discussing values with management. We have various initiatives which regularly provide co-workers with the opportunity to participate and contribute to these discussions.

I So, does culture affect IKEA's recruitment process?

MD It has a major impact. Although it's important for us to get highly skilled people into the company, we're not interested if there's a conflict of value systems. Anyone expecting a flash car or status symbols has no future with us. Recruitment at IKEA's an extensive process, based on judgements about a candidate's value systems and attributes. We can add retail skills, no problem, but it's tough to change someone's mindset.

I Does that go for career advancement too?

MD Yes, it does.

I So Swedish managers will always have more chance of promotion then?

MD We find that many Scandinavians identify more easily with our culture but there is no written or unwritten rule concerning the nationality of senior managers. It would be impossible, however, for anyone to advance within IKEA without wholly understanding and buying into the company's philosophy and culture. So every year senior managers are invited to an annual business meeting in Sweden where they are updated on plans and presented with the new range of products.

I And finally, Ingvar Kamprad stepped down as President in the mid-80s, replaced by Anders Moberg. What effect did this have on the development of IKEA's culture?

MD Both Moberg and the Chief Executive, Mikael Ohlsson, have worked closely with Kamprad for many years and have a deep knowledge and understanding of Kamprad's original vision and philosophy. Naturally, IKEA is different today than it was then, primarily because it is three times bigger and has entered many more diverse and challenging markets. But our values and mission – to provide quality, affordable products for the majority of people – remain very much in situ.

Listening 2 (1.26–1.30)

Speaker 1
We organise anti-bureaucrat weeks, where all the managers have to work in the store showrooms, warehouses or restaurants for at least one week a year. The managers also have to work very hard at IKEA. In fact, the pace is such that we sometimes joke about 'management by running around'.

Speaker 2

The company's very informal. We dress casually and believe in a relaxed, open-plan office atmosphere. In countries like Germany and France, for example, we use informal terms of address such as 'du' and 'tu' rather than 'sie' and 'vous'. But this kind of environment actually puts pressure on management to perform because there's no security available behind status or closed doors.

Speaker 3

Ingvar constantly bypassed formal structures to talk directly with front-line managers. And whenever he visited a store, he tried to meet and shake hands with every employee, offering a few words of praise, encouragement or advice as he did so.

Speaker 4

Our entire east European strategy was mapped out by Ingvar on a small paper napkin. Just about every aspect of the entry strategy was laid out on this small piece of paper – we call it his Picasso. And for the past few years we've just built on and expanded that original version.

Speaker 5

There's also the story about Ingvar driving around town late one night checking out hotel prices till he found one economical enough. I've no idea whether it's true or not but I guess it's all part of the aura and the legend surrounding the man.

Unit 7a: Industrial espionage

Listening 1 1.31

J = Jill   O = Oliver   R = Rick

J   Good morning. Sorry I'm a little late. How did the board meeting go yesterday?
O   I didn't know there was a board meeting planned for yesterday.
R   There wasn't. It was an emergency meeting.
O   Emergency? Sounds exciting. What's the problem?
R   That's what we're here to talk about this morning. Close the door, would you Jill?
J   Yes, of course.
R   Thanks. Right, as you may know, we've lost several major contracts this year to Centronics, our biggest rival. Each time they've targeted the customer just as their contracts were up for renewal.
J   Are you saying they've somehow got access to our files?
R   Well, one of our customers was still loyal enough to inform us that Centronics seemed to have good information about the terms and conditions of their contract with us.
O   But surely, you don't think that someone's passing on that kind of information?
R   We don't know. That's the problem. And that's what we've got to find out. If there genuinely is a problem, then we'll have to find out whether Centronics has infiltrated us or whether it's an inside job. So, we need to look at our systems and our people – and that's why you're both here.

Listening 2 1.32

O   So, what did you have in mind, Rick?
R   Well, first of all, Oliver, could someone have hacked into our intranet from outside?
O   Hack into the intranet? I doubt it. We've got pretty up-to-date security on the system.
J   Which means it's probably an inside job, right? Any ideas who it might be?
R   If I knew that, we wouldn't be here. So, we'll need to check out everyone who's joined us in the last twelve months.
J   The last twelve months? You don't think Centronics has placed a spy here, do you?
R   I'm not sure what to think, Jill. But we should check out their CVs anyway.
J   But it'll take ages if we do that. Besides, their references would have been checked at the time anyway.
R   I know, but what about their previous employers? Were they checked?
J   Well ... we ... we don't normally ...

R   Exactly. I think it'd also be a good idea if you looked back at your appraisal records. See if you can find anyone who's disgruntled or making noises about wanting more money ...
J   Do you mean for the whole company or just Sales?
R   Well, start with Sales and then keep looking if you don't find anything. We've got to be thorough on this one. The board's taking it very seriously. Oliver, on the systems side of things, what can we do?
O   Well, I guess the first thing is to look at access. You know, see who's got access to what information.
R   Could you report back to me on that as soon as possible?
O   Sure. And I suppose I could also issue individual passwords so ...
R   That's true. And then we'd know exactly who was logging on, wouldn't we?
O   And what they were looking at – and when they were logging on.
J   How about email? Can we check people's email?
O   No problem, it's all automatically archived on the server. I'll get print-outs for you, Rick.
J   And if I could see them, too, I could see who's dissatisfied and have a look at their appraisal notes and their personal record file.
O   OK.
J   That way I should be able to get an idea as to whether anyone's bearing a grudge.
O   Good idea, Jill. OK, do that. But make sure you do it discreetly. If word got out about this, then whoever's doing it would stop and destroy the evidence.
J   That's true. It wouldn't do much for morale either.
O   Which is already low enough around here at the moment.
R   Yes, this isn't exactly what we needed right now, is it?
J   What if we don't come up with anything, what are we going to do then?
R   The board's thinking about bringing in a security consultant. She'd pose as a temp in the Sales Department – you know, talk to people and get the gossip, find out who's unhappy and that kind of thing.
J   But I don't see the point. How would she be able to find out anything that we couldn't?
O   And it'd certainly go down well in Sales if they found out about it.
R   Yes, well ... Let's just hope it doesn't come to that.

Unit 7b: Business ethics

Listening 1.33–137

I suppose, in a way, it's a kind of generation thing. When George started, there was no such thing as political correctness in the office environment. In those days, I'm sure it was common practice to call colleagues 'love' or 'darling', pay compliments about their figures or even give them gifts and things. But you just can't do that nowadays and he should have known better. He says his secretary never complained about it to him in person and that if she had, he'd have stopped doing it, but she didn't. Instead, she went straight to the board and warned them that she'd take legal action if nothing was done about it. Well, they soon hauled George in and explained the situation. George was outraged and told them what they could do with the job there and then.

If you'd looked around the workplace, I guess you would have seen the evidence. I mean, in a company of this size you would have expected to see at least some ethnic diversity in the workplace, wouldn't you? Anyway, someone finally discovered a secret file with all the applicants who were not given an interview. Whoever it was blew the whistle to the local press and that was it – the company was faced with a PR disaster and a police investigation. Of course, the first thing the board did was give the well-paid HR executive his marching orders and insist that it was his prejudice and not company policy. But if that was the case, then why hadn't they noticed what was going on?

I'm sure Sharleen didn't think she was doing anything wrong at the time. She'd been told to put together a report on the market penetration of a new safety product we'd just launched. So she had to find out how much business our main rival was doing. OK, so hacking into their corporate intranet wasn't the right way of going about it – but no-one realised she was a complete whizzkid. Luckily, they didn't find out what happened. If they had, it would have cost us a fortune. You can imagine everyone's reaction when she announced what she'd done. Our Ethics Officer went mad and had to quickly put together an official code for dealing with competitors. As for Sharleen, well, she just got away without even so much as an official warning!

We'd been doing business with them for years and our sales executives had always enjoyed very good relationships with them. I don't think for one minute it would have made any difference if we hadn't offered them the occasional thank you for their business. But we always thought of it as good customer relationship management. What's wrong with the odd weekend away for a loyal customer? Anyway, the new CEO changed all that. Maybe it was a cultural thing, I don't know, but she suspended all freebies pending a review. She also recruited someone to regulate dealings with our clients – a sort of moral policeman, I guess. She even wrote to all our customers warning them not to accept any kind of presents from any of our reps.

Every business wants to be ethically sound but it's a hyper-competitive world out there and when you're under pressure to make money and keep to a budget, it's a different matter. Pete, the Production Manager, didn't like the new regulation spray paint – it just wasn't as good – so he carried on using the old stuff. He knew there'd be trouble if anyone found out. But I guess he just hoped they wouldn't. Of course, some campaigners tested the local water and found evidence of the banned chemicals. I suppose when you think about the PR nightmare that followed and the hefty fine the company had to pay, Pete was lucky to get away with just a letter threatening dismissal if he used the old paint ever again.

Model answers to Ex 4, page 117

 (1.38) 7b One-minute talk: How to encourage ethical behaviour from employees

Figures show that more and more companies are now reporting their ethical performance and it's clear I think that companies now have to address the issue of ensuring ethical behaviour amongst their staff. The question is of course – how?

To begin with, awareness is key. The company needs to set out an official code of ethical practice and ensure that all employees have access to it and can understand it easily. The company then needs to implement an effective and anonymous system of reporting any breaches of this code. Once these procedures are in place, the company can then benchmark its ethical practice against those of industry leaders and see how it's doing. I think it's also vital that companies ensure that their senior managers set a good example, 'walk the talk' so to speak. If they don't behave ethically why should staff?

And finally, the company needs to put ethics high on the training and staff development agenda. It needs to make staff understand why ethics is important not just to the company but also to them as well.

 (1.39) 7b One-minute talk: The importance of ethics in today's business world

Well, today globalisation is allowing companies to source from ever greater distances. This enables a company to exploit the economic advantages of low labour costs in one country and high market value in another.

Of course, they have to be careful not to be seen to be exploiting the workers. Consumers are becoming ever more sensitive to the exploitation stories and indeed environmental issues. This is because as consumers become richer and become used to spending more on a product, they also feel that they should be spending ethically. This is backed up by media stories and press items, and exploitation stories receive very good press. And of course, they can cause great damage. The bigger the brand, the higher the risk of a PR disaster.

Also companies are now having to worry about PR among their own employees. After all, recent stories about fat cat executive salaries can easily affect morale and thus workers' productivity.

Unit 8a: Global brands

Model answers to Ex 3, page 125

 (1.40) 8a One-minute talk: The importance of a global presence

With more mergers and acquisitions than ever before, I think it's becoming quite clear that a company in the future will need to have a global

presence in order to compete in tomorrow's market place. This presence can give a company many competitive advantages.

To begin with, say, it can give access to local market knowledge, which can avoid some very, very expensive mistakes on account of cultural conflicts. What's more, it can spread the risk of doing business. If a company sells to more than one market, it can survive a downturn in any one of those markets, that's quite clear. And if a company becomes truly global, it can move its production around from country to country and take advantage of the best conditions at any given time. And the size of the company means it can realise economies of scale in advertising or distribution or shipping, for example.

So I think, all in all, when these things are taken into consideration, it's quite clear that any company not looking to establish a global presence in future may not have a future.

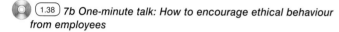 **(1.41) 8a One-minute talk: How to promote an imported brand**

With so many people these days making a conscious decision to buy domestic products, the pressure on those companies wishing to promote imported brands is greater than ever before.

Initially, a company needs to show how their product is superior to the local equivalents. Maybe it's better quality; maybe it's more stylish. A company needs to show customers the benefits of being more adventurous in their buying decisions to encourage them to move away from the current products they use. If you market a product as something exotic or unusual, you're bound to attract new clients. Cultural stereotypes are also a powerful selling tool. A cosmetics range associated with French chic, for example, is bound to attract customers. And if people are looking to buy a reliable car, there's no better label than 'made in Germany'. These national associations can also be exploited at the point of sale. Playing French music in supermarkets, for example, is proven to improve the sales of French wine.

Basically, if you want to successfully promote an imported brand, you need to give your customers a good reason to try something a little bit more exciting than their own home brands.

 (1.42) 8a One-minute talk: The importance of stereotypes in advertising

Well, stereotypes are useful to advertisers because they're basically a shorthand. You've got thirty seconds to get your main selling point across. And with a stereotype you can establish a theme in two.

A stereotype is consistent and easily identifiable to a whole national group. When a German audience see a Scotsman in a kilt, they instantly know that the ad is going to be about economy. And they can make us feel good about our own value systems or customs. We might pit a refined Englishman against a brash New Yorker and that'll give the impression that the product we're selling is obviously full of taste and discretion. And of course, in this way, stereotypes are often identified with positive qualities. For example, the German Audi designers in white lab coats are obviously obsessed with perfection. And so we can guarantee that any product we buy from them is going to be designed to perfection.

And lastly, stereotypes make good comedy because everybody wants to laugh at other countries and people who are different. And of course, if they've had a laugh, they're more likely to remember the advert.

Unit 8b: Global sourcing

Listening (1.43)

I = Interviewer   C = Craig

I   We keep hearing all about the globalisation of markets and supply chains and so on but why has global sourcing suddenly become so widespread?

C   Well, I think there are several factors, really. I mean, as companies expand internationally their outlook becomes increasingly global. What's more, hyper-competitive domestic markets have driven companies to look further afield in their search for competitive advantage. Although I think the process has really been accelerated by rapid advances in IT and telecoms. That's been the real catalyst for change.

I   And what's the great attraction? Why are companies so keen to source abroad?

C   It depends on the circumstances of the company in question. It could be anything from better access to overseas markets, lower taxes, lower labour costs, quicker delivery or a combination of any of these.

I   But it would be fair to say the financial benefits are the main incentive, wouldn't it?

C   In most cases it probably would, yes. Without them, I suppose few companies would be that interested. But there are risks involved as well, you know.

I   And what are those risks?

C   Well, the most common mistake companies make is they only see the savings and don't bother to think about the effect on other key criteria like quality and delivery. A clothing company that only buys from Asian suppliers at low cost, for instance, will find that as labour rates increase over time, it'll have to island hop to find new low cost sites. And this, of course, introduces uncertainty about quality – and that's critical for a clothing company. There are other possible risks as well.

I   Such as?

C   Well, such as negative publicity as a result of poor working conditions in the supplier's country. And, of course, there's always currency exchange risk.

I   So how do you go about weighing up all these factors and choosing a supplier?

C   It's crucial that companies know precisely what they're after from a supplier and that they fully understand their key selection criteria. They need to be careful to define them and make sure they're measurable and then rank them. It's dangerous selecting a particular supplier just because they happen to deliver outstanding performance in one objective such as cost or flexibility.

I   So, having selected a prospective partner, what then?

C   Well, then you have to negotiate how closely the two parties need to work together. If it's going to be a long-term relationship, you need to discuss how much sharing of information and resources will be necessary to extract maximum value from the collaboration. The prospective partners need to sit down and decide on the best form for the relationship to take.

I   And what's the most common form of this relationship?

C   Well, once again it depends on individual circumstances. The relationship can be anything, I suppose, from complete ownership through strategic alliances to buying the market.

I   Buying the market? What's that?

C   That's when companies just publish their specifications and ask prequalified vendors to bid for the contract. General Electric is currently doing $1bn of business this way over the internet. It's a short-term deal with almost no interaction with the supplier and the length of the bidding process is cut by half. But most importantly for companies like GE, order processing is $5 an order as opposed to $50 when it's done on paper.

I   You mentioned strategic alliances. When do they make sense?

C   Well, for an aircraft manufacturer like Boeing, for example, an alliance with its engine manufacturers is logical because of the complex interaction between the body of the aircraft and its engines. And this complexity means everything has to be developed together. The arrangement also has the added bonus of reducing the financial risk of long-term development programmes.

I   And how about actually owning the supplier, then? When is that preferable?

C   Well, companies take over suppliers when they're vulnerable to fluctuations in the availability of key supplies. Take Du Pont, for example, the chemicals giant. Since oil is a primary ingredient of many of its products, Du Pont is very much affected by the availability, and therefore cost, of oil. Du Pont reduced these uncertainties by purchasing Conoco, its main oil supplier.

I   Thus keeping its costs down.

C   Possibly. Owning the supplier definitely increases financial control of the supply chain. But when you take the cost of acquisition into account, there are no short-term savings.

I   So, all in all, does global sourcing make sense?

C   Well, there are lots of very powerful benefits but managers have to consider all the main operational factors very carefully first.

Unit 8: Exam practice <small>(Exam focus CD)</small>

Listening Part One

Good morning. First of all, thank you for inviting me to talk about our electronic meetings system. I've got a handout to give you at the end. But please feel free to make notes.

So, what is DecisionMaker®? Well, quite simply, it enables you to conduct meetings either face-to-face or remotely using networked computers. Now, you're probably wondering 'What's the point of using computers?'. Well, the point is that unlike traditional meetings, everyone gets the chance to contribute because they communicate through the keyboard. This means people can communicate openly with no fear of criticism. And believe me, that can make a big, big difference.

So what are the key advantages of DecisionMaker®? Well, first of all, there is simultaneous input, meaning that everyone 'talks' at once – although electronically, of course. This produces lots of contributions as the process draws on the creative energy of the whole team – not just individuals. Also, because ideas are submitted anonymously, people are free to 'think the unthinkable'. Now this may not sound like much, but believe me, it's a fantastic way of promoting innovation within your company. It also means that all ideas are the property of the team – which is a great boost to team spirit. And each suggestion is evaluated on merit and not on feelings towards the person who came up with it. Imagine that. A meeting without any personal politics.

With DecisionMaker®, ideas belong to the group. This means they are analysed objectively without personal feelings interfering with the way they are developed or rejected. Thus ideas are processed far more quickly than in traditional meetings. And with everyone getting involved at the same level, there is no domination of the proceedings by one or two strong characters. What's more, because the meeting's conducted on computers, everything is automatically recorded so there's no need for a secretary to take notes or minutes. But of course, the real beauty of the system is that you don't need to be in the same place – or even the same country – to hold the meeting!

So, how does it work? Well, let's look at some of the key features of DecisionMaker®. First of all, there's the Whiteboard®, which makes drawings produced during the meeting available to everyone else in the group. Pen passing and free-for-all drawings are also supported. Next we have FileShare®. With this function, the distribution of documents among the team couldn't be easier. Whether it's a spreadsheet, report or graphic image, just drag it into the FileShare window and it's accessible to the team. Thirdly, Consensus® gives instant feedback on suggestions by using one of three voting methods. There's the 10 Point Scale, Yes/ No, and Agree/Disagree. Once more, all votes are anonymous so honesty is guaranteed. And finally, there's Briefcase®, which lets you access your favourite applications during the meeting. If you want to use things like your calculator, your calendar or notepad, simply drag them into the Briefcase and they'll be available whenever you need them.

Right, I'd now like to demonstrate just how the system works.

Part Two

I'm quite well organised really so I have no problems dealing with things like credit notes and invoices. What I do find stressful, though, is having to deal with people when they ring up and complain about damaged goods or a late delivery. We're only a small company, you know, so it's up to me and my colleague to sort things out. Although, having said that, my colleague isn't actually that big a help at all. She spends most of her day gossiping to friends, so people can only get through to my extension. It's no good trying to interrupt her either. She just shrugs her shoulders and carries on. It's very irritating, you know.

My new colleague's really nice. She worked in Despatch up until about three months ago, so she's already familiar with all the forms and things we use here at the company. I've started her off on some basic procedures, like paying salaries and dealing with credit control, which means that I can concentrate on preparing for next month's audit. She's doing quite well actually – well, when she finally makes it into the office, that is. It's almost twenty past by the time she's gets in ... and even later if she goes to the canteen to get something to eat first. I think she just goes there for a good gossip with her friends from Despatch, myself.

Well, I sometimes struggle to keep my cool with the Sales Department always on at us to get things moving more quickly. We're busy enough as it is, what with planning and organising operations, scheduling projects and dealing with plant maintenance. It doesn't help having to share such a small space with my boss. Well, we get on all right even though he's quite a tidy person and I tend to leave the place in a bit of a mess. But what really does annoy me is the amount of time I have to spend unjamming the printer or the photocopier after he's been using it. I just find it so inconsiderate of him to leave me to deal with it all the time.

I'm used to keeping records of prices and ordering office supplies, of course, but I never realised there would be so much to the job. I mean, when I think back to the interview, the Personnel Manager didn't mention half the things I'm now doing. I've never had to actually select the suppliers myself before. It's a real balancing act, getting the right product at the right price. But my colleague's given me lots of useful information. In fact, there isn't much he hasn't told me. We took a break together on my first day here and he didn't waste any time telling me all about everyone in the office. It makes me wonder now what he's saying behind my back.

It's been a real nightmare lately. We're busy enough at the best of times. And now we've lost our admin assistant, it's even worse. I've been up to my neck in paperwork, going through contract details with the Legal Department and checking CVs and references. You know, I've interviewed forty applicants this week already for one of our vacancies and it's only Wednesday today. My colleague seems to take everything in his stride, though. If he's not standing next to the fax machine chatting to someone from the Purchasing Department, he's outside my window smoking. Look, there he is, lighting up again. I can't believe it. That's his sixth one this morning. Honestly, it's a wonder he gets any work done at all.

Part Three 🔊 2.10

J = Jim   S = Sally

J Welcome to Working Hours. In studio today we have Sally Michaels, HR Director at ZSV Insurance, one of many companies promoting flexible working schemes. Hello, Sally.

S Hello, Jim.

J So, Sally, what made ZSV decide to move away from the rigid nine to five?

S Well, social changes have been a major factor. More women are now returning to work after having children, for example. And, even more importantly, we've had to cater for changing customer demands. With customers now preferring to do their business over the phone, we need our staff to work more flexible hours. We also took over two smaller companies recently. So we wanted a common scheme to unite all our new employees.

J So what are the advantages of the scheme for ZSV?

S Well, for one thing, we put great emphasis on providing our staff with regular, high quality training. It costs a lot of time and money to train our employees. So, obviously, it makes sense to retain them.

J And providing them with flexible working patterns can help you do that?

S That's right. But that isn't the main benefit. We see the scheme as primarily a tool for attracting potential staff to our company – especially high-calibre graduates.

J Speaking of your staff, what's the main attraction for them?

S Well, the majority of people in the scheme want to spend more time improving their qualifications by doing an MBA or something like that.

J I imagine the scheme must make it much easier for staff to look after their children too.

S Yes, that is an added benefit, as is being able to dedicate more time to their outside interests, such as sports.

J Now, I believe the scheme isn't totally new.

S That's right. There was an old scheme but awareness of it was very low. Most men, for example, assumed it was only available to women, which, of course, wasn't the case. The new scheme will also continue to offer alternative working patterns to staff on both short and long-term contracts. Only this time, we're making it available to employees at all levels of the organisation and not just people in more junior positions.

J I see. And what do you think will be the most popular element of the scheme? Flexible hours?

S It's difficult to say at the moment but, yes, flexitime is likely to be popular. Typically, though, with the old scheme, employees showed

most interest in having longer breaks from work, and I expect it'll be the same this time. There might be some interest in, say, job share arrangements in the future. But we'll have to wait and see.

J And ZSV is also encouraging teleworking, I believe.

S Yes, we are.

J Now, how does that work? Do you use video-conferencing, for example?

S Well, we have the facilities but they're not that widely used at the moment. As most of our teleworkers have access to the company network, they tend to communicate electronically. It's far more convenient than telephoning because you don't have to worry about whether the person's available or not.

J That's interesting. But what about your managers, what challenges do they face working from home?

S Well, several have mentioned the need to be self-disciplined, differentiating between work-time and private time. But the biggest difficulty seems to be empowering others to act for you, especially when they're in the office and you're not.

J That's surprising. I would have thought the most difficult thing would be staying motivated without the support of colleagues.

S Well, that's not something that's come up so far but I'm sure it will.

J So, how do employees get selected as teleworkers?

S Well, it all begins with an interview with your line manager.

J To discuss whether the home environment is suitable, you mean?

S Well, it's not quite as simple as that. The main reason we have the interview is to ascertain whether the applicant's duties are compatible with working from home. It's easier, say, for an IT specialist to work from home than a PA. If the interview goes OK, we then introduce the applicant to a colleague with personal experience of teleworking. We think it's important for the applicant to hear what it's really like working on your own at home.

J Well, I'm afraid time's running out so we'll have to stop there. Thank you, Sally, for joining us today.

Answer key

Unit 1a: Work roles (Self-study)

Ex 1:
| 1 A | 2 C | 3 C | 4 C |
| 5 A | 6 B | 7 A | 8 C |

Ex 2: *Suggested answers:*

1 The company has just set up a new job share system.

2 He was given feedback on his performance during his job appraisal.

3 Her job description didn't outline her main duties and responsibilities very clearly.

4 I'm really enjoying my new job.

5 The employees carried out the job as soon as they were given their brief.

6 WorkSet was used to classify and highlight aspects of the job.

7 One of the most important things in this job is the ability to communicate.

8 We need to monitor the way he carries out his job.

Ex 3:

2 It was suggested that some training should be/ be organised for our team leaders.

3 It was decided that a consultant should be brought in/be brought in/to bring in a consultant.

4 It was found that team leaders' roles are not/were not clear enough.

5 It was agreed that we should start/we start implementing WorkSet the following month.

6 We recommend that Ekstrom should set up/sets up/set up new assessment centres.

Ex 4:

2 hold
3 says
4 aren't/are not delegating
5 doesn't/does not seem to be getting
6 's/is even bringing
7 think
8 I'm/I am definitely getting

Unit 1b: Company structure (Self-study)

Ex 1:
2 virtual team	3 corporate intranet
4 line manager	5 business environment
6 hierarchical organisation	7 online support
8 operating costs	

Ex 2:

Verb	Noun	Adjective
standardise	standardisation	standard/ standardised
diversify	diversity	diverse/ diversified
respond	response/ responsiveness	responsive
operate	operation	operating

suit	suitability	suitable
supervise	supervision	supervisory
vary	variety	varied

Ex 3:
1 remote	2 sequential	3 virtual
4 specify	5 back up	6 interaction
7 challenge	8 impact	9 email
10 motivation		

Ex 4:
| 1 into | 2 for | 3 under |
| 4 on | 5 with | 6 on |

Ex 5:
1 Correct	2 those	3 such
4 Correct	5 have	6 Correct
7 lot	8 Correct	9 themselves
10 Correct	11 and	12 the
13 Correct		

Ex 6:

2 've/have just promoted

3 hasn't/has not even been working **or** hasn't/has not even worked

4 did she join

5 told

6 saw

7 's/has broken

8 's/has been looking

9 thought

10 was

11 's/has made

12 have already been calling

13 's/has he taken **or** did he take

14 didn't/did not mention

Unit 1: Exam practice

R1:
| 1 D | 2 C | 3 B | 4 E |
| 5 A | 6 B | 7 E | 8 C |

R5:
1 their	2 from
3 how	4 on
5 a	6 the
7 is	8 more
9 up	10 such

Unit 2a: Stocks and shares (Self-study)

Ex 1:
1 peak	2 level off
3 general upward trend	4 fluctuate
5 bottom out	6 recover

Ex 2:
1 shares	2 flotation
3 broker	4 investment
5 listings	6 commission
7 merger	8 dividends

Ex 3:
1 Neutral	2 Positive
3 Negative	4 Positive
5 Negative	6 Negative
7 Positive	8 Neutral

Ex 4: *Suggested answer:* *(133 words)*

This year, April sales of Fresh 'n' Cool reached 725,000 units, which was slightly down on last year's total. May saw sales fall to a new low of 700,000 units before they began to make a recovery in June. Sales rose steadily to peak at 1.3m units in July. However, in August, they fell slightly, to 1.25m units.

In contrast to this spring's poor performance, last year's sales showed strong growth between April and July, rising from 750,000 to over 1.25m units. However, they then fell sharply in August, finishing back at their April level of 750,000 units.

Therefore, although sales of Fresh 'n' Cool were initially down on last year's figures for the same period, they actually had a much stronger finish this year equalling last year's July peak of 1.25m units.

Ex 5: *At the start of 1996, shares in Octavian Cotton stood at $160. However, by the end of the year they **had collapsed** to just $50. They recovered **steadily** over the next twelve months but **fluctuated** sharply all through 1998. In 1999 they continued their **recovery, climbing** to $160 per share, where they remained throughout 2000.*

*Shares in Minchin Textiles starting trading at $150. Like Octavian, Minchin saw **its** shares fall during 1996 and then **pick up** the following year. This recovery then **turned** into a general upward trend, **which** continued until late 1999, when shares peaked at $220. They then collapsed before **rising** briefly to just over $150 at the end of 2000.*

Unit 2b: Mergers and acquisitions (Self-study)

Ex 1:

Acquired another company	Merged with another company	Was acquired by another company
Lloyds TSB	BP	HBOS
RBS	Glaxo Wellcome	ABN Amro
HSBC	SmithKline	Household
Vodafone	Beecham	International
		National
		Westminster Bank
		Mannesmann

Noun + noun or adj + noun	Prefix + noun
long-term	sub-prime
hat-trick	mega-mergers
fee-paying	re-establishing
Empire-building	
deal-makers	
self-interest	

Ex 2:
1	takeover	2	merging
3	growth	4	competitive
5	benefits	6	streamline
7	restructuring	8	acquisition

Ex 3:
2 integrate different cultures
3 add long-term value
4 undercut competitors' prices
5 reduce operating costs
6 generate cost improvements

Ex 4:
1	to	2	represents/is
3	that	4	its
5	whether	6	not
7	while	8	such

Ex 5: The merger raises a number of HR issues (1) **which/ that** will need to be addressed as a matter of urgency and in a manner (2) **which/that** is seen to be fair to the employees of both companies. Firstly, the pay structures of the two companies, (3) **which** show marked differences, will need to be reviewed and harmonised. Furthermore, redundancy terms will have to be agreed and offered to employees (4) **who/that** lose their jobs as a result of the merger. This is particularly important with regard to senior managers (5) **whose** contracts contain severance clauses (6) **which/that** guarantee them generous terms. Our approach to these job cuts, (7) **which** were promised to shareholders as part of the terms of the merger, will also have a major effect on staff morale within the newly-formed company. It is imperative that we avoid any deterioration of staff morale, (8) **which** could have an adverse effect on company performance.

NB: If **which** or **who** can be replaced by **that**, no comma is used.

Unit 2: Exam practice

R2:
1 D		2 C		3 E	
4 F		5 G		6 A	

R4:
1 C		2 B		3 A		4 C
5 D		6 C		7 A		8 D
9 B		10 B				

R5:
1 had		2 what		3 as	
4 out		5 many		6 such	
7 no		8 all		9 which	
10 their					

R6A:
1 order		2 a		3 been	
4 Correct		5 which		6 Correct	
7 in		8 the		9 but	
10 Correct		11 be		12 you	

R6B:
1 they		2 Correct		3 Correct	
4 have		5 Correct		6 that	
7 of		8 Correct		9 to	
10 a		11 make		12 for	

Unit 3a: Trade fairs (Self-study)

Ex 1:
1 a		2 Correct	
3 Correct		4 do	
5 Correct		6 which	
7 Correct		8 it	

9 these   10 Correct
11 and   12 Correct
13 are   14 Correct

Ex 2:

```
1 a d v e r t i s e m e n t
        2 r e p l y
3 a p p l i c a t i o n
            4 d e s i g n
      5 e v e n t s
    6 b e n e f i t s
        7 s t a n d s
      8 r e t a i l e r s
9 b r o c h u r e s
```

Ex 3:
2 With reference to your letter of
3 We look forward to meeting you
4 Further to our conversation of
5 Should you have any further questions
6 Please do not hesitate to contact me

Ex 4:
2 lands
3 get
4 arrive
5 will take / is going to take / is taking
6 have checked in
7 get
8 go

Unit 3b: Entering a market (Self-study)

Ex 1:
seminars
trip
association
practices
norms
card
acquaintance
negotiations

Ex 2:
1 invest in	2 intend to
3 amount to	4 build on
5 allow for	6 participate in
7 respond to	8 enquire about

Ex 3:

make	do	enter into
conversation	a mailshot	a joint venture
an investment	business	a partnership
a request	research	a relationship
a commitment	preparatory work	

Ex 4:   *Suggested answer:*   *(130 words)*

Doing business in London and Beijing

Looking at the overall situation, it is far cheaper to do business in Beijing than in London. The most dramatic differences can be seen in the cost of office space and salaries. Renting office space is currently ten times cheaper in Beijing than in London. Likewise, a

bilingual secretary in Beijing earns barely a tenth of the going rate in London. The cost of a local phone call in China is more reasonable than in the United Kingdom, a five-minute call being approximately 25% cheaper in Beijing, as is the average cost of accommodation at a five-star hotel. The single area in which Beijing outstrips London in terms of cost is rent, with the price almost double that of a comparable property in London.

Ex 5:
2 forge relationships
3 pledge investment
4 produce trade literature
5 swap business cards
6 provide hospitality
7 start proceedings
8 match needs

Ex 6: At meetings with **the** Chinese, **the** leader of your group will be expected to enter first and will generally be offered **a** seat beside **the** most senior Chinese person present. This person will usually chair **the** meeting and act as **the** / --- host. At **the** beginning of **the** meeting, all **the** people present will greet each other and swap business cards, after which **a** period of small talk begins. **The** host will then officially start **the** / --- proceedings with **a** brief introduction to **the** Chinese enterprise. **The** visiting team is then invited to speak. It is appropriate at this point for foreign participants to make their case and answer questions. Following **the** meeting **the** Chinese enterprise will probably arrange **a** special dinner for **the** overseas guests along with other entertainment such as sightseeing. Guests should always accept these invitations as small talk in **a** social setting is essential for forging relationships with **the** Chinese.

Unit 3: Exam practice

R3:
1	B	2	C
3	D	4	D
5	B	6	A

W2:   *Suggested answer:*   *(229 words)*

Dear Mr Salter

Re: Reference for Mr John Bridge

Further to your letter dated 15 October, I am writing concerning the application of John Bridge for the position of Training Manager at STC International.

I have known John for over fifteen years, and feel that the length of our friendship, together with my personal experience of working as Training Manager at Tarbus UK, allows me to comment on his suitability for the advertised position.

As you are aware, John is currently employed by Tarbus UK as Training Co-ordinator for the busy Marmouth branch, where his main responsibility is to assess the training needs of the employees and arrange training programmes to meet these needs. This involves liaising with a large number of language and business skills organisations as well as evaluating the effectiveness of the training employees receive.

John has excellent interpersonal skills and is sociable, patient and a good listener. As a friend, I particularly appreciate his loyalty and sense of humour. I also admire the calm and logical way in which he approaches difficult situations.

I have no hesitation in recommending him for the position of Training Manager for your company and wish him every success in his application.

If you have any further questions, please do not hesitate to contact me, either at the above address or on (01420) 655567.

Yours sincerely

Julia Shipton
Training Manager

Unit 4a: The future of work (Self-study)

Ex 1:

1	Negative	2	Positive	3	Negative
4	Negative	5	Positive	6	Positive

Ex 2:

1	C	2	A	3	B
4	A	5	B	6	A
7	B	8	C		

Ex 3:
2 foster team spirit
3 key a number into a telephone terminal
4 run out of supplies
5 show interest
6 centralise operations
7 adapt to a new way of working
8 vacate premises

Ex 4:

1	between	2	on	3	on
4	to	5	into	6	on

Ex 5: meet needs, spend time, run a meeting, predict needs, suit needs, hold a meeting, waste time

Ex 6:
2 It is unlikely that the office will cease to be important.
3 The internet looks set to explode.
4 More people are bound to want to work from home.
5 It is improbable that everyone will have an iPad®.
6 Working from home will undoubtedly increase in future.

Unit 4b: e-business (Self-study)

Ex 1:

1	no / little	2	their	3	that / how	4	but
5	such	6	the	7	any	8	which / that

Ex 2:

	1	i	n	t	e	r	n	e	t			
	2	w	e	b	s	i	t	e				
				3	b	u	l	l	e	t	i	n	s
	4	t	r	a	n	s	a	c	t	i	o	n	s
		5	o	n	l	i	n	e				
			6	i	n	t	r	a	n	e	t	
	7	i	n	t	e	g	r	a	t	e		
	8	b	r	o	w	s	e	r				
		9	c	u	s	t	o	m	e	r	s	

Ex 3:
2 manage inventories
3 improve operating efficiencies
4 handle transactions
5 communicate with partners
6 analyse customer behaviour
7 personalise offerings
8 anticipate customer wants

Ex 4:
2 after-sales service
3 product support
4 staff turnover
5 customer base
6 distance learning

Ex 5: *Suggested answers:*

2 We'll be doing more online training in future.

3 She won't have finished the report by the end of next week.

4 We won't be using any paper invoices next year.

5 He will have completed the website by July.

6 I'll be rethinking our internet strategy over the next few weeks.

7 Internet usage will have doubled within 5 years.

8 We won't be launching the products until the website has been completed.

Unit 4: Exam practice

L1:

1	1975	2	popularity
3	suitable premises	4	rapid expansion
5	substantial contracts	6	resources and knowledge
7	high-street chemist	8	new factory
9	brand name	10	marketing operations
11	family atmosphere	12	market leader

L2:

13	D	14	B	15	C	16	E
17	G	18	N	19	K	20	J
21	L	22	M				

L3:

23	A	24	C	25	B	26	B
27	C	28	A	29	A	30	A

R4:
1	B	2	C	3	D	4	A
5	C	6	A	7	D	8	A
9	B	10	C				

Unit 5a: Staff motivation (Self-study)

Ex 1:
1	being	2	which
3	Correct	4	Correct
5	such	6	Correct
7	of	8	any
9	Correct	10	those
11	certain	12	Correct
13	the	14	Correct

Ex 2:
1	ineffective	2	insignificant
3	unsatisfactory	4	irregular
5	unappreciated	6	inflexible
7	irresponsible	8	uninteresting
9	incapable	10	unspecific

1	unappreciated	2	incapable
3	interesting	4	specific
5	irregular	6	ineffective
7	inflexible	8	irresponsible

Ex 3:
2	restore	repair
3	schedule	plan
4	appreciate	value
5	sever	cut
6	rename	rebrand
7	address	deal with
8	quit	resign

Ex 4:
1	into	2	from	3	towards/to
4	behind	5	of	6	as

Ex 5:
2 are awarded
3 are not based
4 has been criticised
5 was introduced
6 have been noticed
7 will be/is going to be reviewed
8 are currently being encouraged
9 is also provided/has also been provided
10 can be found

Unit 5b: Recruitment (Self-study)

Ex 1:
1 The client instructs the headhunter to fill a vacancy.
2 The headhunter identifies possible candidates.
3 The candidates are interviewed by the headhunter.
4 The headhunter provides a shortlist of candidates.
5 Candidates go through the client's selection process.
6 The client appoints one of the candidates.
7 The client pays the headhunter his completion fee.

Ex 2:
2 extension number
3 future reference
4 executive search
5 neutral location
6 key player

7 sensitive information
8 skills shortage

Ex 3:
1	on	2	on
3	for	4	into
5	to	6	across
7	in	8	with
9	to		

Ex 4:
2 present findings
3 shortlist candidates
4 pay a retainer
5 conduct business
6 compile a list

Ex 5: *Suggested answers:*

1 The recruitment agency claims there is an acute skills shortage in the IT sector.

2 For recruitment purposes we need an up-to-date copy of your CV.

3 Advertising a job vacancy in newspapers is one recruitment method; using an agency is another.

4 If you're looking for a job, why not apply to a recruitment agency?

5 When recruiting new staff, we look for evidence of exceptional past performance.

6 I have shortlisted candidates with the qualities which we know to be necessary from our previous experience of recruitment.

7 Before he was appointed, he had to go through the client's internal recruitment process.

8 Using a headhunter to recruit a new employee can save a company time.

Ex 6:
Verb	Noun
apply	**application**
appoint	appointment
compare	**comparison**
explain	**explanation**
categorise	category
recruit	**recruitment**

Ex 7:
2	which	3	its
4	which	5	those
6	which	7	This
8	who/that	9	this/such
10	these/the		

Unit 5: Exam practice

R1:
1	B	2	C	3	E	4	A
5	D	6	C	7	B	8	E

R5:
1	which	2	unlike
3	however	4	only
5	each	6	a
7	such	8	both/each
9	one	10	than

Unit 6a: Corporate culture (Self-study)

Ex 1:

1	A	2	A	3	B	4	C
5	C	6	B	7	A	8	A

Ex 2:

1	adaptations	2	competitors
3	operations	4	promotional
5	interpretations	6	expansion
7	influential	8	perceptive

Ex 3:

2	similar	alike
3	informal	casual
4	fresh	new
5	economical	thrifty
6	vital	crucial
7	tough	hard
8	global	worldwide

Ex 4:

2	arriving	3	operating
4	restructuring	5	working
6	(to) increase	7	realising
8	to be	9	to let
10	believe	11	confronting
12	to turn	13	to reflect
14	looking	15	modernising
16	to be		

Unit 6b: Cultural diversity (Self-study)

Ex 1:

1	means that	2	However
3	while	4	therefore
5	as opposed to	6	although / while
7	Similarly		

Ex 2: *Suggested answer:* (133 words)

Mustermann AG and Svensson AB

The graph shows the changing number of employees at Mustermann and Svensson from 2006 to 2010. Looking at the general trend, there has been an upward movement in the number of employees at Svensson whereas Mustermann has seen numbers fall dramatically over the same period.

During 2006 and 2007 there were 175,000 employees at Svensson. Employee numbers rose steadily over the following three years to reach 210,000 in 2010.

On the other hand, from 2006 to 2009 Mustermann saw employee numbers fall from 230,000 to an all-time low of below 175,000. In 2010, however, Mustermann felt sufficiently confident to start taking on new employees once more with the result that by the end of the year employee levels stood at 185,000, slightly higher than the figure for 2008.

Ex 3:

2 fix salary levels
3 conduct a meeting
4 appreciate differences
5 build understanding

6 solve a dilemma
7 follow a strategy
8 hold a belief

Ex 4:

Verb	Noun
choose	choice
succeed	success
expect	**expectation**
affect	effect
pay	**pay / payment**
believe	**belief**
solve	solution
promote	**promotion**
diversify	diversity
examine	**examination**
preserve	preservation

Ex 5:

2 We needn't have gone there.
3 We shouldn't have adapted the product.
4 We ought to be getting back.
5 The language problems can't have helped.
6 They might be having trouble working together.

Unit 6: Exam practice

R3:

1	A	2	C	3	C
4	D	5	B	6	B

W2A: *Suggested answer:* (226 words)

Report: Cost-cutting: Administration Department

Introduction
The aim of this report is to examine ways of cutting costs in the Administration Department and explain the implications of these cuts for the running of the department. It is based on the results of a detailed questionnaire sent to all employees.

Findings
It is clear that within the department there are a number of areas where cost-cutting measures could be taken. The most significant areas of concern are the following:

● *paper*
● *refreshments.*

Recommendations
In order to deal with the issue of paper, it is suggested that the department installs a system to recycle all used printing and photocopying paper. It is expected that by adopting new recycling procedures, the department could save as much as £100 a month.

As for refreshments, it is recommended that tea and coffee should only be offered free to employees during morning and afternoon breaks. At all other times employees should be required to pay for refreshments. This measure should reduce the company's monthly bill for refreshments from £320 to £110, thereby making a saving of over £200.

Conclusion
It is felt that the above measures will result in immediate and substantial savings for the Administration Department. Although these recommendations are

not expected to affect the running of the department in any significant way, managers should be prepared to encounter initial resistance from staff.

R4:

1 D	2 C	3 C	4 A
5 A	6 B	7 B	8 A
9 B	10 D		

R5:

1 is	2 although/while
3 with	4 what
5 not	6 for
7 both/all	8 the
9 as	10 few

W2B: *Suggested answer:* *(247 words)*

Dear Mr Schommartz

Re: Work placement at Shiptols UK,
  1 Feb 2000–31 July 2000

Further to your appointment as Trainee Public Relations Assistant, I would like welcome you to Shiptols UK. I would also like to take this opportunity to provide you with some introductory information, both about the company itself and the duties you will be expected to perform during your time here. I trust you will find the following points useful.

Unlike many of our overseas subsidiaries, Shiptols UK is divided into seven main departments: Production, Research and Development, Finance, Personnel, Sales, Marketing and Public Relations. I work in the Public Relations department, which is headed by Jenny Holloway. Public Relations is the smallest department in the company, consisting of fifteen employees, who usually work in teams of five. As my assistant, you will generally report directly to me.

My job mainly involves communicating with our local distributors. However, I am currently in charge of organising a major press launch for our new 'Easywash' washing powder, which is due to take place on 15 April. Initially you will be working with Claire O'Reilly, who is responsible for designing the information packs for the press launch. Your duties will include helping to write articles for the pack and choosing photographs for inclusion.

I look forward to working with you in the near future. In the meantime, if you have any further questions, please contact me on (+44) 1431 23776.

Yours sincerely

Martin Wallis
Communications Officer

Unit 7a: Industrial espionage (Self-study)

Ex 1: *Examples of industrial espionage:*
infiltrate a competitor, bug an office, hack into a network, leak sensitive information, steal confidential data, resort to shady practices

Measures against industrial espionage:
monitor photocopier use, shred important documents, bring in a security adviser, identify a perpetrator, protect a computer system, install passwords

Ex 2:

1 Correct	2 this	3 of
4 to	5 been	6 Correct
7 Correct	8 Correct	9 who
10 Correct	11 by	12 Correct
13 a		

Ex 3:

Verb	Noun	Adjective
accept	**acceptance/acceptability**	acceptable
suspect	**suspect/suspicion**	**suspect/ suspicious**
imitate	imitation	**imitation**
access	**access/accessibility**	**accessible**
analyse	**analysis**	**analytical**
secure	security	**secure**
protect	**protection**	**protective**
copy	copy	**copiable/ copied**
identify	**identity/identification**	**identifiable**
confuse	**confusion**	**confused/ confusing**
isolate	**isolation**	**isolated**
break	**breakage/breach**	broken
measure	**measure/measurement**	**measurable**

Ex 4:
  2 call the police
  3 bear a grudge
  4 devise a system
  5 break the law
  6 suspect foul play
  7 shred paperwork
  8 take measures

Ex 5: *Suggested answers:*
  3 're/are
  4 can go
  5 's/is
  6 'd be/would be
  7 could also look
  8 can give
  9 like
  10 doesn't have/does not have
  11 do you still want
  12 didn't find/did not find
  13 doesn't/does not need to
  14 's/has
  15 's found/has found
  16 'll put

Unit 7b: Business ethics (Self-study)

Ex 1: *workplace safety, sexual harassment, racial discrimination, conflict of interest, environmental issues, product safety, competitive practices, privacy, executive salaries, gifts and entertainment/ corporate gift-giving, corporate philanthropy, whistle-blowing, legal compliance, fair employment practices,* delivery of high quality goods and services, industrial espionage, financial mismanagement

2	sexual harassment	3	workplace safety
4	legal compliance	5	executive salaries
6	corporate gift-giving	7	racial discrimination
8	whistle-blowing		

Ex 2:

1	illegal	2	unethical
3	unfair	4	unlawful
5	incorrect	6	unofficial

Ex 3:

2	measure	precaution
3	conduct	behaviour
4	rule	regulation
5	threat	warning
6	rival	competitor
7	freebie	gift

Ex 4:

1	who	2	to
3	more	4	did
5	when	6	on
7	that	8	as
9	else	10	a
11	when	12	'd/had

Ex 5: *Suggested answers:*

2 The boss would have sacked him by now if he weren't the Managing Director's nephew.

3 If we hadn't got that contract, the company wouldn't have survived the recession last year.

4 I'm sure she would have been dismissed if anyone had found out how she was getting her information.

5 If she hadn't been filmed shredding the files, she'd still be working here today.

6 The problem would have been solved more quickly if the company had brought in a consultant earlier.

7 The company wouldn't have known if the new assistant hadn't blown the whistle to the press.

8 If he'd left sooner than he did, the company wouldn't be having all the bad publicity it is right now.

Unit 7: Exam practice

R2:

1	C	2	E	3	A
4	G	5	D	6	B

R6:

1	Correct	2	the	3	which
4	with	5	Correct	6	and
7	that	8	what	9	Correct
10	you	11	Correct	12	a

W2: *Suggested answer:* (240 words)

Report

Working conditions

Introduction
The aim of this report is to assess the main reasons for staff complaints about working conditions and propose ways of improving the situation. It is based on the results of a detailed questionnaire sent to all employees in addition to in-depth interviews with managers and union representatives.

Findings
As might have been expected, low pay is the main reason for staff complaints. Furthermore, a significant number of employees are not satisfied with the current level of bonus payments and fringe benefits. Another major complaint is the employees' working environment. In particular, poor ventilation and lighting in communal areas such as the canteen and coffee room have been highlighted.

Recommendations
In order to deal with the issue of pay, it is recommended that a meeting should be arranged with union representatives to discuss both a review of pay levels and the launch of a range of incentive schemes. This could, for example, lead to the introduction of performance related top-ups, with bonuses being awarded to those employees who exceed a target level of performance per week. In addition, employees who have been with the company for over two years could be entitled to a range of fringe benefits, such as subsidised private health care arrangements. It is also suggested that employees are offered an opportunity to express their views on improving their working environment by using a Suggestions Box, which could be put in the canteen.

Unit 8a: Global brands (Self-study)

Ex 1:

1	cultural	2	advertising
3	globalise	4	adapts
5	production	6	universally
7	diverse	8	profitably

Ex 2:

1	with	2	towards
3	with	4	to
5	round/around/on	6	as
7	from		

Ex 3:

2	busy	hurried
3	essential	vital
4	domestic	national
5	cosmopolitan	diverse
6	robust	strong
7	classic	traditional
8	beneficial	advantageous

Ex 4: *Suggested answer:* (140 words)

Report: Comparison of Serabi and Shanta Gold shares

At the start of the period Serabi and Shanta Gold share prices were both 33.50 pence. Yet, by the middle of February Serabi shares had reached 41 pence while Shanta Gold's had fallen slightly.

By mid-March both companies saw their share prices fall. Shanta Gold shares fell steeply from 33 pence to 28 pence, rising briefly before falling to a low of 26.50 pence. Prices picked up by the end of March and continued to show an overall upward trend finally reaching 32.5 pence in May, slightly lower than their price in early February.

Serabi's share price, however, following the sharp fall in March, picked up and increased steadily until mid-April by which time they had recovered to 38 pence. From then onwards there was a steady decrease in the price, reaching a low of 28.5 pence in early May.

Ex 5:
2 spending power
3 target market
4 global presence
5 creative concept
6 marketing campaign

Ex 6:
2 Rarely are our advertisements translated.

3 Never before has it been easier to advertise globally.

4 On no account should cultural differences be ignored.

5 Only in Europe have we had any success with it.

6 Under no circumstances should we change the logo.

Unit 8b: Global sourcing (Self-study)

Ex 1:
1 B	2 C	3 B	4 A
5 B	6 C	7 B	8 B
9 A	10 C		

Ex 2:
1 No	2 No	3 No	4 Yes
5 Yes	6 No	7 Yes	8 No

Ex 3:
2 warranty   guarantee
3 attraction   incentive
4 reputation   image
5 plant   machinery
6 premises   buildings

Ex 4:   *Suggested answer:*   *(137 words)*

Unemployment in Italy and Germany, 1993 to 1998

General trend
Unemployment figures in both Italy and Germany rose significantly over the period from 1993 to 1998.

Italy
Despite an overall increase, the unemployment figures were characterised by number of peaks and troughs over the six years. In 1993 unemployment stood at just over 9% of the total workforce, rising to 12% in 1995. It then fluctuated around this level until 1998, never falling below 11.5%.

Germany
In contrast, unemployment in Germany rose steadily with far fewer fluctuations, increasing from 8.5% to almost 10% by late 1993. Despite an improvement the following year, with the level falling to just under 9.25%, the upward trend continued, with unemployment reaching a peak of 11.5% by the end of 1997. However, 1998 saw unemployment drop sharply to 10.7% before levelling off.

Ex 5:
1 were confirmed
2 its
3 the
4 to win
5 who
6 had been holding out
7 had taken place
8 would have created
9 will not be releasing
10 are likely to
11 have also been circulating
12 announced
13 would be
14 are cutbacks feared
15 are made

Unit 8: Exam practice

L1:
1 networked computers	2 fear of criticism
3 creative energy	4 innovation
5 on merit	6 analysed objectively
7 no domination	8 secretary
9 drawings	10 distribution of documents
11 voting methods	12 favourite applications

L2:
13 E	14 C	15 G	16 D
17 H	18 J	19 L	20 P
21 O	22 M		

L3:
23 B	24 B	25 C	26 B
27 C	28 A	29 A	30 B

R4:
1 C	2 D	3 B	4 C
5 A	6 A	7 D	8 C
9 D	10 B		